BV 29 .C8 1956
Cummings, Oliver De Wolf, 1900-
The Youth fellowship : a vital church
program for youth.

THE YOUTH FELLOWSHIP

THE COOPERATIVE SERIES
LEADERSHIP TRAINING TEXTS

Many thousands of lay workers in Protestant churches attend interdenominational leadership education schools each year. It is essential that the courses offered and the text materials used be acceptable to the many varieties of Protestant groups found in our American communities.

The Cooperative Series of leadership education textbooks are produced to meet that need. They are planned by the Division of Christian Education of the National Council of the Churches of Christ in the U.S.A., representing thirty-nine Protestant denominations. The Cooperative Publication Association, an interdenominational group of denominational editors and publishers, selects the writers and provides editorial supervision to insure sound educational values, practical usefulness, and interdenominational approval and acceptance.

A COOPERATIVE TEXT

The
YOUTH FELLOWSHIP

A Vital Church Program for Youth

by OLIVER DeWOLF CUMMINGS

PUBLISHED FOR
The Cooperative Publication Association
by
THE JUDSON PRESS

CHICAGO   PHILADELPHIA   LOS ANGELES

BV
29
.C8
1956

THE YOUTH FELLOWSHIP

Copyright, 1956

by

THE JUDSON PRESS

All rights in this book are reserved. No part of the text may be reproduced in any manner without permission in writing from the publisher, except in the case of brief quotations included in a review of the book in a magazine or newspaper.

The Scripture quotations in this volume are from the Revised Standard Version of the Bible, copyrighted 1946 and 1952 by the Division of Christian Education, National Council of the Churches of Christ in the U.S.A., and are used by permission.

This is one of a series of books produced for interdenominational use by the Protestant denominations working through the Cooperative Publication Association. It is a recommended text for Course No. 312B in the Standard Leadership Curriculum of the National Council of the Churches of Christ in the U.S.A.

LIBRARY OF CONGRESS CATALOG CARD NO. 56-9297

PRINTED IN THE U.S.A.

Dedicated to my father
SELDEN W. CUMMINGS
warmhearted father, minister, professor
exemplar of Christian fellowship
friend and counselor of youth

"What shall be the course of society and civilization across the next hundred years? For the answers read if you can the strange and baffling eyes of youth. Yes, for the answers, read, if you can, the strange and baffling eyes of youth."

— Carl Sandburg, in *Always the Young Strangers*. Copyright, 1952, 1953, by Harcourt, Brace & Co. Used by permission.

"YOUR YOUNG MEN SHALL SEE VISIONS"

We can have a dynamic Christian youth movement in America if we want it badly enough. We can have churches with vital youth programs, and youth with vital Christian experience. But this will take effort. First, we must make good use of the extensive resources of the Christian church. It has millions of youth, many needing to come face to face with God and to respond to the call of Christ. There are many capable adults whose lives may find fulfillment as friends and counselors of youth. Then, there is the Christian gospel itself, waiting to be released upon the world as a force to heal, to inspire, and to uplift.

There is sufficient "know-how." Are we willing to acquire it? There are tested ideas and plans ready to be used. Are we willing to put them to work? There is literature enough for study, inspiration, and guidance. Shall we give it an honest trial? God himself is available. Are we?

The trouble is, we have been holding out on God. The time has come to give him our best. We who have used our God-given powers to manufacture and distribute millions of machines to operate farms and factories; to build skyscrapers and bridges; we have a rendezvous with another opportunity. We can, if we will, furnish the brain power and the skill, the creative imagination and resourcefulness, to enlist youth for God.

For this task the most urgent need is for good, honest workmen in each local church — young people and adults who will team together in a friendly partnership. We need clear Christian aims, willing minds and spirits, and enough knowledge to sense where to begin and what to do next.

7

THE YOUTH FELLOWSHIP

This is an appeal — to young people, to adults who work with or might work with youth, and to ministers. It is an urgent invitation to give the Christian Youth Fellowship a chance, by whatever name it is called in your church. It is a challenge to invest something of yourself in an adventure of discovery — so you may build, not on hunches, but on solid and tested experience.

I have written about the Youth Fellowship because I firmly believe in it. I hope you share this faith, or will find yourself doing so as you read. Whether you work in a rural or an urban church, with junior highs, senior highs, employed older youth or students, the Youth Fellowship in its varied expressions has much to offer. First of all, find out what its characteristics and potentialities are. Don't allow it to become stereotyped and tame. Keep it fresh and alive, as is the gospel itself. And use the Youth Fellowship — not as an end, but as a means — to kindle flames in the hearts of youth, and to light Christian fires in your own community and around the world.

My undying appreciation is expressed to many colleagues — young people and adults — who have shared their ideas and experiences during the years prior to, and following, the development of the Youth Fellowship movement in which I have lived and worked with them in local, state, and national church leadership. I am especially grateful for close associations with young people in camps and retreats, and in the manifold activities of the Youth Fellowship and the United Christian Youth Movement. To many of these persons, I can point as living evidence and say, "Here is proof that the 'fellowship idea' works."

— OLIVER DEWOLF CUMMINGS

Los Angeles, California
March 1, 1956

CONTENTS

9

CONTENTS

10

Contents

CHAPTER I

PUTTING THE FELLOWSHIP IDEA TO WORK

"We, though many, are one body in Christ, and individually members one of another." [1]

IT IS SUNDAY MORNING at nine-thirty. The place is Our-town, U.S.A. The group includes fifteen young people from the local high school. The meeting room — once a part of the church basement — now is attractively decorated, with two smaller sections for classes, which serve also as work areas for many projects. The young people fixed it up themselves and feel proud of it.

There's a spirit abroad in this group. They sing as though they mean it. They discuss matters frankly but with a sense of respect for one another. They meet here often. This morning it is for worship and Bible study. Tonight it will be for discussion. The meetings differ in type, but there is a central purpose which seems to run through all that is said and done. These young people take seriously their faith in God and their loyalty to Christ and the church. Between Sundays there are committee meetings, planning sessions or workshops, and parties. Frequently two or three drop in for table games, to make a poster, to write letters, play records, or just to talk. They have had lots of fun here, and have done some real work. But this morning they are doing serious thinking about the Bible and about their own lives. Somehow all of it is caught up in what is called the *Youth Fellowship*.

In separate rooms, the Junior High Fellowship and the

[1] Romans 12:5.

13

Senior High Fellowship are meeting with quite different activities but similar spirit. What *is* the Youth Fellowship? What are its objectives? What is its program? How is it organized? How is it administered? What are the secrets of its success? Let's see if we can find out!

WHAT'S THE BIG IDEA?

There *is* a big idea behind the Youth Fellowship movement. Each adult leader and each youth member should have a clear understanding of this idea and of the basic principles which apply to youth work in local churches. This big idea centers in an emphasis upon fellowship — a spiritual experience of individuals and of a group.

The name "Fellowship" for the church youth group is well chosen. In its richest and fullest sense, it is an important word in the Christian's vocabulary. The New Testament says, "We have fellowship with one another" (1 John 1:7). This spiritual bond is a clue to an understanding of the nature of the Christian life and of the Christian church. To be a Christian is to have fellowship with God, to come to know him through responding to the call to accept Jesus as Savior, and to follow him as "the way, the truth, and the life." To be a member of the Christian church is to share with others this experience of fellowship — in worship, study, recreation, witnessing, serving, and giving.

The big idea back of the Youth Fellowship has two aspects: For the individual it says that *Christian personality,* based on fellowship with God through Christ, *is central;* and for the group it insists that the *Christian church,* that is, the Christian fellowship, *is the basic loyalty of life.* We shall seek to discover in this book the practical implications of this idea, and the basic principles upon which to build youth work in the church.

14

WHAT DIFFERENCE DOES IT MAKE?

It does make a great difference how young people approach church work, what they expect of it, and more particularly what they feel it demands of them. Church work with youth must be more than a reflection of the secular culture and activity which surround the church. The church has a different and higher mission.

Let the church be *the church.* Let it be famous for that for which it is unique — *Christian fellowship.* Young people may experience genuine association with God and with one another. Through this association they may come to know the true nature of the divine-human fellowship which is the Christian church. The desire to apply its spirit to everyday relationships at home, school, or job can make a difference in nearly everything a young person does. And it can greatly change the spirit, the procedures, and the accomplishments of the youth group as a whole.

It's important right at the beginning to do a little thinking about youth work as it now is and as it once was. We need to know how we got where we are and discover where we intend to go from here.

HOW DID WE GET WHERE WE ARE?

"How does it happen," says a junior high boy, "that the young people's groups in the different churches in our town have similar names and organizations?" This question deserves an answer.

First, one of the most exciting and significant developments of recent years in the Christian church is the Youth Fellowship movement. The name "Fellowship" is used in many denominations. Other denominations organize their youth work along similar lines but under different names.

Millions of young people are now related to churches in which the name Youth Fellowship is officially used for the church's youth groups. Other millions attend churches where the "fellowship idea" is in large degree operative, though under other names.

Think of the potentialities wrapped up in all these Youth Fellowshipers. What a thrill to be a part of such a youth movement! Our chief interest is in the *idea,* not the name. This book will have meaning for all youth groups, no matter what may be the name they use.

Youth work has had quite a history. Before the development of the Youth Fellowship, a state of affairs existed in the churches which was quite chaotic. Several organizations competed for the loyalty of youth with overlapping functions, gaps unprovided for, and with limited co-ordination. Wherever a new need arose, a new organization was developed — with a limited objective, but usually with a full quota of officers and committees.

The church youth program in Ourtown looked like this. We had the Sunday church school, with its organized youth classes (using such class names as Baraca, Philathea) . . . the Sunday evening "young people's society," with separate officers . . . the missionary organizations for girls, and in some denominations, for boys . . . also the Boy Scouts, Girl Scouts, Camp Fire Girls, Hi-Y, athletic clubs, and many others. And often the co-operation between all these separate organizations was very poor.

Gradually, a simpler and more effective approach of the church to its youth work was discovered. In one denomination after another, steps were taken to establish an improved organizational pattern — the Youth Fellowship. In these developments, young people themselves, lay leaders of youth, ministers, and national officials have had a part. *Now, a*

16

new force, the Youth Fellowship movement, is abroad in America, and the end is not yet.[2]

WHAT'S IT ALL ABOUT?

Basic concepts underlying the Youth Fellowship movement make it much more than a new scheme of organization. The Youth Fellowships have arisen out of a philosophy of Christian education which emphasizes: (1) *the central place of the church* as a true brotherhood of Christian community, and (2) *the sacredness of human personality* as over against an excessive stress upon organization.

The principle of unity

The basic principle upon which the Youth Fellowships are established is that of *spiritual unity* or *oneness*. Part of the task of the Christian teacher is to help young people to discover that the world in which we live is a *uni*-verse created and maintained by one all-wise and all-powerful God. They need to realize that he operates with consistency through one set of physical and moral laws. These are not subject to whims and caprice, but apply universally and in all ages. A sense of unity and oneness underlies the Christian life, the Christian church, and the Youth Fellowship — for "we . . . are one body in Christ."

Personality comes first

According to the Christian gospel, in all God's universe with its immensity of size, its complexity of structure, and its almost infinite variety of objects, animate and inanimate, *there is nothing more sacred than personality*. It is in this realm that Christ most perfectly revealed the nature of God.

[2] For a more extended discussion of the Youth Fellowship movement, see *Orientation in Religious Education*, P. H. Lotz (ed.), Abingdon-Cokesbury Press, 1950; chapter entitled, "The Youth Fellowship," by Oliver deW. Cummings.

It is for this — *personality,* as expressed in human beings — that Christ died. One of our tasks is to help young people to respect personality, in themselves and others, as God's most precious and eternal gift.

It is appropriate, therefore, that the Youth Fellowship should be founded upon the principle that personality should come first, as an end in itself, never a means. This points up the fact that organization and activity always should be kept secondary.

The church is central

If the church of today and tomorrow is to be strong, youth must be helped to understand the uniqueness of the church among all human institutions, and must be taught to believe in it and to give themselves to its divine purposes. The Youth Fellowship emphasizes this central place which the church should occupy in the life of youth. The Fellowship conceives of itself as being a real part of the church. It is concerned deeply with the ultimate spiritual purposes for which the church exists.

The church is unique in that it is divinely established, and has a divine mission — to lead men to God, and to help them express in personal living and in human relationships the true nature of the eternal God as revealed in Jesus Christ. *The church is not merely an organization; it is a living organism* — "the body of Christ" — in which each separate member is a part of the whole. Young people need the feeling of strength that comes from the sense of belonging to this institution of which there is but one true leader, Christ. They must believe so deeply in the uniqueness of the church that they are eager to assign to it first place in their affections and to devote to it their highest powers. The unbelievable sacrifices of war must be matched by the unrestrained dedication of Christian discipleship. Thus, youth will stand ready to work with Christ to accomplish his goal: "I will build my church, and the powers of death shall not prevail against it."

Fellowship is basic

Nothing is more necessary for human beings than fellowship. This is particularly true of young people, whether as early adolescents they are arriving at a conscious awareness of their need for group associations or as later adolescents they are alert to problems of social adjustment. To be sure, the Youth Fellowship has a mission to provide an opportunity for boy to meet girl, for young people to have fun, to make friends and influence people. But, much more, the Fellowship should be the expression of the highest relationship for which the church exists — man's spiritual association with God and with his fellows. In the Youth Fellowship at its best, the ideal spirit of Christian comradeship finds expression in all the varied activities of worship and study, work and play.

The church itself is a fellowship

A Christian church is more than an organization — *it is a fellowship*. It is a part of the family of God. It is a family of families in which each member is important. All share privileges and responsibilities, joys and sorrows. And the strong help the weak. This is a redemptive institution which has been founded on love and which is concerned about growth.

The church itself is a school of Christian living, a brotherhood of disciples. Jesus himself commissioned us with the words, "Go therefore and make *disciples* . . . teaching them to observe all that I have commanded you."

19

In every relationship of life — family crisis, school club, athletic contest, job flare-up, or individual temptation — young people may be sustained by "the tie that binds," the sense of belonging to the church, a loving fellowship that is seeking to be Christlike.[3]

HOW BIG HAS THE FELLOWSHIP IDEA BECOME?

The "fellowship idea" itself has had growth. It is now big in its numerical and geographical scope, embracing all parts of the country and a great majority of the young people of all races and cultural backgrounds in the Protestant denominations. There is inspiration in this knowledge. Great potentialities exist in the ideas and resources available through community, regional, and national sharing. The "fellowship idea" is also big in its possibilities for the local church. It comes close to the heart of what the church is, and it includes all aspects of the church's program for youth. Here is *one of those big ideas which may indeed revolutionize the life and spirit of the church itself.*

WHO'S INCLUDED?

The Youth Fellowship, as the youth division of the church, includes *all* the young people of the church *whenever* they meet. This applies Sunday morning to the church school class or department, Sunday evening to the youth meeting, and weekdays to youth events or social functions. The lower age level is usually set at approximately *twelve years,* more particularly *seventh grade.* The upper age level varies in different denominations and local churches, usually approximately *twenty-three to twenty-five years.*

[3] Adapted, in part, from *Guiding Youth in Christian Growth,* by Oliver deW. Cummings. The Judson Press, Philadelphia, 1953. (For further discussion of the implications of fellowship as applied to Christian teaching and belief, see that text, especially Chapters I and II.)

WHAT ARE ITS PRACTICAL IMPLICATIONS?

A unified program

Since the goal is to create unified Christian personalities, there should be *one program,* with diversified activities so co-ordinated as to develop full, rounded Christians. There should also be *one leadership,* with enough youth officers and adult counselors and teachers so that too great a burden will not fall upon the president and chief adult adviser. The curriculum, the activity program, and the organizational functioning should be so planned as to meet the needs of growing persons and to build a sense of group solidarity centering in the church.

One primary loyalty—to Christ

The Christian movement offers to youth an allegiance to the highest in the universe — to the God who is supremely revealed in Christ. As the early disciples were joined together in a living, dynamic, expanding whole by their faith in Christ as their matchless Leader, so the youth of our time may transcend national and racial divisions and may be linked together as an irresistible force for world transformation by their allegiance to Christ. More than anything else in life, each individual young person needs the creative and unifying factor in his own experience which can be supplied only by a deep and abiding loyalty to Christ as Leader. *The Youth Fellowship substitutes for loyalty to many organizations and leaders one overshadowing loyalty — to Christ.*

One ultimate organization—the church

There should be but *one ultimate organization for the Christian — the church itself.* The youth activities should be so conducted as to emphasize the primacy of the church. This is done through one organizational sub-unit for each age group (junior highs or intermediates, seniors, older youth) which is inclusive of all young people and all activities of the church for that particular age group.

This organizational unit, whatever its name — whether known as the Youth Fellowship or by some other name — should create a growing sense of allegiance to those things for which the divine institution, the church, was created. These include worship, study, evangelism, missionary endeavor, Christian service, and fellowship. The curriculum should include study of the church and its missionary achievements. The leaders of the local church should be known, and their tasks understood. The church's responsibilities and activities should be shared by youth. They should feel themselves to be a real part of its fellowship.

Many churches have been challenged to greater accomplishment by the fresh enthusiasm and insight of their younger members. For example, one youth group, after participating in a denominational conference, attended the annual business meeting of their church and convinced those present that they should increase the missionary budget of the year by a substantial figure, which they then helped the church to raise.

The youth division of the church

In other words, the Youth Fellowship is simply the youth division of the church. This means that the aims of the young people should be essentially the same as those of the church, though adapted to their special capacities and needs. It also means that young people should undertake to meet some of the church's problems and needs, should be prepared for places of leadership in the church, and should give systematically to its local and world program.

HOW DOES IT WORK?

Does it apply to small churches?

In thousands of small or medium-sized churches, the Youth Fellowship is an established fact. It is not necessary that the numbers be large. As few as five young people have functioned well as an effective Youth Fellowship in many churches. The age range may of necessity be spread widely. The desire to work helpfully with others — even though of different ages and interests — is inherent in the very spirit of fellowship. In such cases the older and more mature seek not to dominate but to assist the younger and less mature in personal growth. If the number is small, the organization should be kept simple, but it is quite feasible to have a comprehensive, well-balanced program.

Wherever numbers permit, it is advisable to divide into two age-group fellowships: for example, a Junior High (or Intermediate) Fellowship and a Senior-Older Youth Fellowship.

Is it flexible enough to meet varied situations?

One of the great assets of the Youth Fellowship is its flexibility. It adapts itself readily to many situations and groupings. In average and large churches, there is good reason for following, where feasible, the more commonly-accepted groupings, as follows:

Junior High (Intermediate) Fellowship—ages 12, 13, 14; grades 7, 8, 9
Senior High Fellowship—ages 15, 16, 17; grades 10, 11, 12
Older Youth Fellowship—ages 18-23 (24, 25); beyond high school

In some situations there is also a Student Fellowship as a fourth grouping, or as an alternate to the Older Youth Fellowship if the older youth group is exclusively or predominantly composed of students. The single-grade or two-grade groupings (for example, grades 7, 8,) are in existence in some larger churches, and there are single-grade Youth Fellowship classes in many church school departments.

Where do junior highers belong?

Early adolescence (referred to in this book either by the term intermediate or junior high) is a true part of life, not a period of marking time, getting ready for future living. Junior highs like the feeling that they actually do belong to the Youth Fellowship, and that what goes on makes a real difference to them now. Often, it is their interest in their own group and its functions which will coax them into acquiring the skills which are basic to all group life in the church. Such skills, for example, as learning how to

pray in public
read the Bible aloud
give a talk
plan a meeting
take part in a worship service
take part in a dramatic skit
conduct a committee meeting
plan and carry through a project

These skills are acquired through study and practice. So is the knowledge of the Christian faith; so, also, the many skills in personal living and the adjustments to God and to other people which junior highs must make. A comprehensive program of group activity is necessary to furnish opportunity not only for study and training but also for experiencing life on their own level. Junior highs like to have their own organization and officers and to do their own planning, with the help of adult advisers, in an Intermediate or Junior High Fellowship.

24

Where do senior highers fit in?

Middle adolescence (referred to in this book either by the term senior or senior high) is one of the best of all times for effective group functioning in the church. The rich and rounded experiences of an active Senior High Fellowship make large appeal to high schoolers, and furnish training for personal living and for churchmanship which can be provided in no other way. Personality traits are becoming clearer, specialized aptitudes and skills more apparent. Senior highs still need to experiment in making new friends, and to discover potential skills. There is much yet to be learned. Some of this learning began in early adolescence; some of it is quite new. Here are a few examples:

    making a speech
    teaching a lesson
    planning and leading a worship service
    planning and conducting a party
    presiding at a business meeting
    building a calendar of dates and emphases for a year
    planning and producing a play
    leading a song service

Some who have not yet acquired basic skills and shared personally in elementary experiences need to be encouraged to make a start; others, to improve. Knowledge and skills in various fields — music, art, writing, dramatics, handiwork, audio-visuals — need to be lifted to their highest levels and dedicated to the work of Christ.

How about employed older youth?

Later adolescence (referred to in this book simply as older youth or the Older Youth Fellowship) is a highly important time in life. These young people constitute a group essential to the youth program. Here is a span of years, beginning at eighteen — which is twice as long as junior high or senior high spans — during which the preparation for a long span of adult years is reaching its peak.

Older youth are now mature enough to give creative leadership. They may set the pace for their younger brothers and sisters. Yet they still need to learn, and to be associated with the social activities and training opportunities of the youth program. In some respects, those employed are matured by the responsibility and discipline of work; in other respects, those in the universities are matured by the discipline of study; those in the armed services, by military discipline and experience. For all, there is the great challenge of helping to carry through a virile and effective church-centered youth program. As each one reaches full maturity in years or experience, or both, he should be encouraged to become an active factor in the young adult group. In many churches the young adults include a ten-year age span, approximately 25-35.

Prematurely pushing older youth out of the Youth Fellowship is a great mistake — for it deprives them of the privilege of leadership and growth in the youth work of the church, and it undercuts the effectiveness of the youth program. This is particularly disastrous if there is no young adult group for them to join. If a young adult group does exist, it may be weakened by too wide an age span (say, 20-35), or by eliminating on account of age ("too old") many in their early thirties who are properly classified as young adults.

The fellowship idea permits great flexibility with respect to these age groups. Individual preference and local conditions will largely determine the time when a person ceases to be a part of the Older Youth Fellowship. Age is but one of the factors determining whether a person has passed from youth into young adulthood. Among maturing experiences are: (1) *age;* (2) *economic self-sufficiency* — full-time employment; (3) *social freedom* — away-from-home residence; (4) *political maturity* — eligibility to vote; (5) *completion of formal education* — graduation from college; (6) *participation in the armed services;* (7) *marriage.* Many of these categories apply to individuals who are still young and properly belong in the Youth Fellowship. Actually, in great numbers of Older Youth Fellowships throughout the country, many of the most active members have shared in several of these experiences. Marriage is probably the most maturing of all experiences, and is usually accepted as evidence of adulthood. A further factor is that of mind-set, or choice. Where individuals or groups feel that they do not belong in the Youth Fellowship, it is usually better to move them into a young adult group already existing or to create a new one.

What about students?

The Fellowship concepts of the church and of group work are well suited to student groups. The name has general appeal. It implies freedom from organizational rigidity, and indicates the spiritual nature of the group. Student Fellowships now exist in many local churches and on many campuses. Some of these groups refer to themselves by name simply as Student Fellowships; others prefer individual or special names, such as Roger Williams Fellowship, Westminster Fellowship, Wesley Fellowship, and Bethany Fellowship. A number of campus groups do not consciously associate student work with the Youth Fellowship movement, but they would benefit from the realization of a tie-up.

Student work differs widely in various situations. The terminology, program, organization, and activities must be varied to suit these situations. The flexibility of the Youth Fellowship is a great asset. While the concept of group work places primary emphasis upon the church and upon a quality of Christian fellowship, it permits great variation in organization, program, and procedures. The strength of the Fellowship idea, as applied to student groups, lies in the broader unity which transcends differences.

Among different types of institutions of higher learning are the following:

The church-related college (many of these are small, in towns or cities, and have a close tie-up of the student religious program with community churches); the *state university* (usually has a large enrollment; often a high proportion of commuters; a small proportion of students reached by campus-related student religious groups); *graduate* and *undergraduate specialization schools* of many types (some permit little time for extra-curricular activities; meager provision for student religious life) ; *junior colleges,* in a growing number of communities (in many schools supported from public funds, practically all the students commute; the student religious program is carried on largely in the churches).

The students who attend these schools may be classified, in terms of housing, as follows:

1. *Daily commuters* (this group constitutes a large and increasing proportion of the total student population, especially in the large cities). For great numbers of these students, the best way of providing continuous and meaningful Christian fellowship is in relation to the youth program of some church near their residence. This should be supplemented whenever possible by the campus religious group. 2. *Weekend commuters,* returning home a large proportion of the weekends. (Here is a large number of older youth for whom the ties with the home church youth program as well as the campus religious group should be kept as strong as possible.) 3. *Dormitory or fraternity house residents.* Many students share in these situations, permitting a more unified social life and closer association with campus student organizations or with community churches. 4. *Off-campus boarders.* Many students away from home live at varying distances from the campus in private homes or boarding houses, hence need association with other young people in community churches or in campus religious groups.

The number of students unreached by any religious group is so large that all possible resources should be marshaled to meet their needs. Advantages of emphasis upon the Youth Fellowship among students include the following:

1. The Student Fellowship, as a specialized application of the Youth Fellowship movement, may be made flexible enough to include various types of campus or local church student groups.

2. In local churches where students and others are part of the same group, the needs of all may be served in an Older Youth Fellowship.

3. There is great advantage in maintaining the same philosophy of Christian education at graduated levels for pre-college, college, and post-college groups. Thus the Youth Fellowship prepares young people for college, remains with them in college, and equips them to find a place of leadership in the local church youth or young adult group in the crucial years just following college.

4. The policies permit the maximum use of the resources of the church in the interests of students—church buildings and equipment, ministers, lay leaders, and the organized Youth Fellowship channels—national, state, and local—for contacting and enlisting youth. As more and more young people go to college, work with older students becomes as much a concern of each local church as work with high school students.

5. The creative leadership of students during and following their college training is a necessary factor in building a dynamic local church and nation-wide Christian youth movement. To cut students off from this opportunity for leadership is to isolate them in an unreal campus-centered world, to be untrue to their higher needs, disloyal to the church, and unfair to the Christian youth movement in its wider aspects.

6. The Youth Fellowship movement is strongly ecumenical in spirit (i.e., it emphasizes interdenominational and world-wide co-operation) and for this reason makes wide appeal to students and offers channels for their leadership.

What about those in military service?

A disturbing fact about our times is the large number of young people whose lives are upset by military service. Many begin and end their service while still in the age range of the Older Youth Fellowship. Some, when they come back, prefer to take part in the young adult activities; others prefer the Youth Fellowship. The choice seems to depend upon such factors as these: Where are the girls of their own age, and those a year or two younger? Are there fellows of their own age and maturity in the group? How easy is it to "break into the group"? What kinds of experiences have the young people had in service, and how do they feel about the church? To what degree have they been kept in touch by letters and visits when in service? Those using GI benefits to complete their education are usually thrown with younger fellows and girls. The big problem is to reach those who feel strange, out of touch, and uninterested.

While a man is in service, his contacts with the home church, with the Youth Fellowship, and with civilian church groups near the points of service should be kept strong.

An important development is the United Fellowship of Protestants for servicemen. This program came into being because of the desire of men in service for a group similar to the Youth Fellowship which they had known in local churches. Young people should be prepared in their local groups to help the chaplains in establishing and maintaining these groups. Information may be obtained from: United Fellowship of Protestants, 122 Maryland Ave., N.E., Washington 2, D. C., or from denominational youth departments.

WHERE DO WE GO FROM HERE?

In little more than a decade since it was started, the Youth Fellowship dream has become an established force for good in thousands of churches and has influenced millions of lives. It has proved its down-to-earth practicality and its enormous potentialities. But we are just at the beginning. There are beachheads yet to establish, territories yet to conquer. No idea or plan is worth much unless it is put to work with honest effort. The Christian cause, in our day, desperately needs youth and leaders of youth who can dream dreams and make their dreams come true.

The program needs strengthening at a number of points:

1. The ideal of one church-centered program for all youth of each age group is only partially realized in many morning church schools and weekday club sessions. 2. A strong weekday Youth Fellowship program needs to be developed, especially for junior highs. 3. The specialized junior high, senior high, and older youth programs need improvement. 4. The student work needs to be strengthened and brought into closer association with other aspects of the Youth Fellowship movement. 5. A stronger vocational discipleship program needs to be developed. 6. More help is needed in preparing older youth to assume lay leadership responsibilities in the church.

There is also need for expansion and outreach. The youth resources of the churches of America are tremendous, numbering in the millions. Think of what the early church could have done with these. But there are millions unreached in America and around the world. The need is for a manifestation of true Christian fellowship in every church and community so dynamic as to reach with increasing power the youth of junior and senior high schools, colleges, and universities, and rural and urban youth wherever employed or wherever they gather. This Youth Fellowship movement must be realistic enough to make a difference in individual lives and local communities, and world-minded enough to express the Christian faith in all areas of life throughout the world. The problem is to find enough leaders who can inspire enough youth groups in enough towns and cities throughout America to release the resources of God in a mighty movement for world redemption. This book is written in the firm faith that, under God, this can and will be done.

positive

31

AIMS

Chapter II

WHITHER BOUND?

*"I press on toward the goal for the prize of the up-
ward call of God in Christ Jesus."* [1]

THE SPIRITUAL CLIMATE FOR
A VENTURESOME MOVEMENT

Much depends upon the atmosphere in which youth live.
Climate makes for life or death, success or failure. A Youth
Fellowship — like a young plant — may be smothered or un-
dernourished. Or it may be helped to grow and bear fruit
a hundredfold. Human plants may be ruined. Excessive
criticism will do it. Also pessimism, overprotection, adult
domination, lack of faith, failure to supply knowledge and
guidance for growth. Adventuresome movements are often
helped along in the fertile soil of encouragement. Praise will
accomplish wonders. So will constructive counsel, enthusiasm,
understanding, imagination, insight, and, above all, *faith.*
Ministers, counselors, teachers, parents, and youth officers
can do much to help create the right kind of spiritual climate
and soil.

HOW THE FELLOWSHIP SPIRIT IS CAUGHT
AND SPREAD

The Fellowship spirit starts with any young person or adult
who believes in the Fellowship idea and has faith in this
concept of church work with youth. It spreads when this
individual shares his faith in this idea — this spirit — with a
few others; they, in turn, with still others, until finally an

[1] Philippians 3:14.

entire group has been filled with new spirit. Those in the church group may share with youth outside until a community is changed. One group in a community or an area can inspire other groups in other churches of the same community or of other areas. Thus a whole city or county or state may feel the impact. When many groups in many sections catch the spirit and all begin to influence others, a national and international movement is under way. Thus it has always been with the Christian religion.

The Youth Fellowship idea has from the first been spread in this way — because young people and their leaders have believed in it and have put their faith into action.

First, someone must start, often an adult counselor or a young person who has been to camp or conference. But before starting anywhere, it is essential to have some idea where you are going and how to get there.

The chapters which follow on meetings, planning, organization, and program will help leaders to build a functioning Fellowship. This chapter offers specific suggestions on aims. It also shows how the Youth Fellowship may become vital — a dynamic force with a contagious spirit. "According to your faith be it to you," said Jesus.

HOW THE YOUTH FELLOWSHIP PROGRAM IS MADE VITAL

Of vital interest to youth

Many things interest young people — postage stamps, athletics, books, television, dates, food, clothing, worship, science, the nature of the universe, the meaning of life, vocations — to mention but a few. Some of these are more important than others. Since the time at the disposal of the church for specifically religious guidance is limited, it is necessary to choose. Wherever basic interests can be selected this should be done. The skill of the leader comes not alone in the choice of topics but in the ability to lift ordinary discussion or activity to religious levels and discover the Christian implications involved.

It is a mistake to assume that young people are not deeply interested in the truly important issues of life. Though they reject "stuffiness," because it often is a cloak for artificiality in religion, they also reject superficiality, another all-too-common fault. Most young people want reality in religion because true religion deals meaningfully with their most important problems. A vital group is one which deals with the great essentials in a vibrantly alive fashion.

The vital nature of the Christian gospel

The power of the Christian gospel to move youth lies in its vital nature. It deals with the ultimates of life — right or wrong (sin); failure or spiritual success (salvation); the value of life (service to God and man); the meaning of things (the truth); the permanence of life (immortality); the nature of God (absolute love); the meaning of the life and death of Jesus. No leader of youth who wishes to help young people with things which are really vital can afford to neglect these concepts. The problem is to make them understandable to youth, who need help in finding through their own experience the eternal truths which the early disciples felt so keenly. These truths include "the new birth"; "the life more abundant"; spiritual transformation "by the renewing of your mind"; the gospel as "the power of God unto salvation"; "to know Him" as the basis of eternal life; the experience of being "clothed with power." The gospel was and is more than good news; it was and is exciting news. It should be presented in an exciting way.

The vital place of the church in the life of youth

There is terrific competition for youth from a multitude of lesser interests in our secular world. They will not continue in the church unless they discover a truly vital place for it in their life program. This means an awareness that the things for which the church ultimately stands are actually the most vital experiences of life — confrontation with the living God, acceptance of his purposes and plans, genuine worship of him, study and application of Christian truth, acceptance of Christ as Companion and Savior, a unique kind of spiritual fellowship and a commitment to day-by-day discipleship and vocational service. Moreover, not only is awareness necessary but also opportunity must be provided for youth to express his faith in meaningful service. One reason for the effectiveness of Youth Week, as observed annually by many churches, is that young people actually share the responsibilities of the church for one week as officers and board members. The church suddenly comes to life for them.

When youth and Christ get together in a vital program

There is no way of estimating what may happen when youth respond to the leadership of Christ in a program that is truly vital. The encouraging experience of all who have worked long with youth is that the most dynamic and creative young people are often those most completely challenged by Christ and by a vital church program. Again and again young people have been lifted to levels of extraordinary group solidarity and achievement because their minds and hearts have been gripped by the spirit of Christ. The goal of the local leader is twofold: 1. To inspire individuals to become responsible and vital Christians. No one knows when and where another Martin Luther, John Calvin, Roger Williams,

John Wesley, Adoniram Judson, Dwight L. Moody, John R
Mott, Albert Schweitzer may appear to influence the course
of history. 2. To fire the group to manifest an exceptiona
quality of fellowship with Christ and with one another — a:
did the twelve disciples, the early martyrs, the bands of per
secuted Christians in occupied countries in recent years. Such
youth — with Christ — can make a great difference in .every
community.

DISCOVERING WHAT INDIVIDUAL
YOUNG PEOPLE NEED

Every young person is different

Church work with youth should be planned to meet the
needs of young people in particular, not young people in
general. The problem is how to discover the particular needs
One way is through the use of interest-finder charts, question
naires, check sheets or personality profile forms. Each leader
should keep a confidential notebook or file containing check
sheets and other notations on the interests, attitudes, prob
lems, skills, and character traits of each member of the group
It is not necessary to consult a professional counselor or to use
scientifically prepared forms requiring professional appraisa:
in order to get valuable data for use by average persons.

In their book, *Better Ways of Growing Up,* Crawford and
Woodward include many check sheets which Christian young
people themselves may use. For example, one questionnaire
which has often been used lists twenty "Problems That
Trouble Teen-agers":

(1) shyness; (2) nervous habits; (3) nail-biting; (4) speech defects
(5) feelings of inferiority; (6) feelings of differentness; (7) sense of shame;
(8) jealousy; (9) worry and anxiety; (10) unfriendliness; (11) discourage
ment; (12) loneliness; (13) daydreaming; (14) bragging; (15) moodiness
(16) fears; (17) irritability; (18) pouting; (19) sense of failure; (20) sen-

itivity. Questions are included about each problem; for example, under
"shyness": Do I keep to myself too much? Am I afraid to meet people?
Would I rather not go to parties?[3]

Many clues to individual needs will be found in such non-
technical books as *On Call for Youth,* by Wittenberg.

Yet there are universal and typical needs

Though every young person is different, still there are
many needs — primary and basic to life — which all share in
common. These needs include food for the body and food
for the spirit; fellowship with God and with other people;
instruction and moral guidance; release from the sense of
guilt; and spiritual strength for the moral struggle. It is significant that the church is such an important channel for
supplying so many of the highest needs. A young person's
Christian faith is the integrating factor which produces strong
character, and emotional and spiritual maturity.

In addition to universal needs shared by all human beings,
here are typical needs which individual young people may
face. One minister listed the following as he thought of individuals in his youth groups: (1) how to be accepted; (2) how
to overcome feelings of insecurity and inferiority; (3) adjustment to sudden death of a close friend; (4) what to do about
a broken home; (5) family tensions; (6) alcohol; (7) how far
to go on a date; (8) how to get and hold a job; (9) how to get
better grades; (10) how to get to college; (11) how to get help
from prayer. Rowena Ferguson, in her publication *Teen-
agers — Their Days and Ways,* furnishes much insight on
representative needs.

A leader of youth may ask himself such questions as these:
What is it that we expect to have happen to a young person

[3] From *Better Ways of Growing Up,* by J. E. Crawford and L. E. Woodward. Copyright, 1948. Muhlenberg Press, 1948. Used by permission.

who comes to our church and participates in the Youth Fellowship? How does his knowledge grow, his faith mature, and his strength of character increase? Is he helped in his junior or senior high school, or in college? What happens as he faces the problems of clubs, study habits, temptations, military service? Does a junior higher gain self-acceptance, and learn to get along well with others? What about the problems of today's world — social and economic groupings, political issues, community co-operation, race and cultural relations, world peace? How can broad statements of aim be used to measure what's happening?

A good leader knows it is important to define clearly his specific aims in terms of individuals, and to plan each meeting and activity so as to help individuals to reach these goals.

FINDING AIMS FOR THE GROUP

How group goals differ from individual goals

There are also goals for the group which are necessary to its functioning effectively as a true fellowship. These goals relate to such matters as: group spirit — "Are we Christlike?"; collective worship — "Are we aware of God and responsive to him?"; attendance at meetings — "Do we all attend regularly?"; evangelism — "Are we reaching others?"; participation in discussion — "Does everyone take part?"; study and group activity — "Are we all learning and sharing?" Such goals involve a sense of group progress and accomplishment, and assume that there will be group projects in which all share.

The voice of youth—whose goals are they?

The leader needs to be clear that these goals must ultimately become *youth* goals, consciously accepted and desired by his own groups; otherwise, they have no value. It is tragic for a leader to think he is leading a tour and to discover his group has left him to go on another trip. That's why it is so important to encourage goals which originate with individuals in the group, and to take time to make sure that any aims brought in from somewhere else actually "belong" to the group. The plain fact is, we are all so made that we like to feel we are steering our own lives. Young people hate too much "back-seat driving" after beginning to have experience at the steering wheel. To be sure, the leader needs to have destinations of his own — and these may be formulated in his own mind in clear form for his own use. But, if he sees it to be his goal to help young people to arrive somewhere, then he must learn how to share his ideas with youth, and wait for them to be accepted. He should recognize valid insights which did not originate with him. He must *listen for the voice of youth.*

The function of the leader

terrific

In other words, the function of the Christian leader is not so much to stand out in front and give directions. It is to walk in step with youth; to wait for them to discover the way for themselves, if possible; to stand by to assist when help is needed in taking the right fork in the road. The Christian leader is a companion and guide, not a dictator. This conception of Christian leadership applies to youth officers as well as to adult counselors.

The leader may have several different conceptions of his role:[4] 1. He may think of himself as merely a *sitter* — too timid or too bewildered to know how to exercise his functions as a leader. 2. He may regard himself as primarily a *censor* — to squelch irregular or dangerous ideas or conduct, to put

---

[4] These ideas are suggested by flip-chart set, *The Adult Leader and His Youth Group,* copyrighted by John Knox Press.

the brakes on when things get too rough. 3. He may conceive his job to be that of *organizer, administrator, executive* — with his hand *on* everything and *in* everything so that things will go efficiently. 4. He may be interested in being a *good fellow,* popular as a teller of funny stories, a back-slapper and glad-hander. These ideas contain elements of value, yet none of them is adequate. The *ideal leader works and plays, struggles and plans with young people,* so that he is felt to be truly one of them, respected because he has insight and maturity and also because he does not dominate or exploit. He permits young people to make their own discoveries, and displays good judgment and restraint in the amount of advice and suggestion he offers.

Goals for the youth division of the church

Every church needs to have general goals for itself, as a Christian institution, and for its youth division as a whole. Here are some examples: (1) to reach and enlist in the youth program all the young people, ages 12 to 24, who are in the families of the members and in the community served by the church; (2) to develop a program of stewardship of time, talent, and money which will assure adequate undergirding of the task of the church; (3) to provide for better participation in the planning and conducting of meetings and study groups; (4) to develop leadership for the church school and other activities of the church; (5) to develop a program of Christian vocational guidance; (6) to provide a place and a program of recreation for youth; (7) to undertake projects of service in the church and community; (8) to produce an understanding of the Christian faith and such deep commitment to it as to lead to a "redemptive fellowship of youth" expressing itself in the Christian church and in all human relationships; (9) to increase missionary-mindedness.

40

How goals differ—in churches, localities, and groups

Goals for church work with youth differ, and rightly so. They depend upon a number of things. A country church will have different goals, at some points, from those of a city church or will assign greater or less importance to certain aims. A group of employed older youth may be more acutely conscious of job adjustments and human relations. A group of students may be facing intellectual adjustments in a maturing faith. Young people from an apartment-house district may be more in need of church-sponsored opportunities to get acquainted than young people in a compact residential area. Even in the same church, there may be widely differing groups at different times, depending upon home life, early training, personality traits and interests. Denominational goals may include study of distinctive beliefs, practices, and heritage, also special emphases and projects. Each leader should study his own denomination, his own church and locality, and the individual young people in his immediate group. Goals should be formed that truly apply.

Formulating a covenant or group statement of purpose

It might be desirable for a group of young people to incorporate their goals in a covenant or a group "Statement of Purpose." Such a project might well be made the basis for discussion in a meeting or in a series of meetings. Such points as these might be discussed: "What we stand for"; "What makes our Christian youth group distinctive"; "What we feel God expects of us"; "What we are trying to do and be." The discussion could start off with a review of the question, "What are the things which are really important in establishing a vital Christian youth group?" This would lead to listing on a blackboard, or in the notebook of a "recorder," such general items as prayer, worship, Bible study, church loyalty, Christian service, consistent living, witnessing, Christian conviction. The group might like to discuss each of these in some detail, and perhaps formulate broad statements under general headings, such as: "These are things we believe" (about God, Jesus, the church, the Bible, the future, etc.); "We accept these disciplines" (daily prayer, Bible study, witnessing, systematic and proportionate giving); "We covenant to do these things" (regular attendance at church, at youth meetings, witnessing, a regular place of service).

The more originality the group can put into such a statement of purpose, or covenant, the better. If comprehensive statements, such as those which follow in this chapter, are to be used for comparison, it is better to wait until the group has done its own thinking. The effort may be made to produce a balanced document, brief enough so that it may be lettered up for a wall chart, and carefully enough worded to carry continuing inspiration. After general discussion an editorial committee may be assigned the job of improving the wording. This locally developed statement of purpose will have uses different from those of nationally formulated covenants (such, for example, as that of the Methodist Youth Fellowship).

ORGANIZING AND GROUPING GOALS FOR PRACTICAL USE

The statement of aims of Christian education

A classic study of aims in Christian education was made by Paul Vieth and incorporated in his book, *Objectives in Religious Education*. This study has served as the basis for the formulation of goals by the Department of Education of the National Council of Churches and by co-operating denominations. In various modified forms it has wide general use. The major headings may be stated as follows:

Christian education seeks to foster in growing persons —

(1) a consciousness of *God* as a reality in human experience, and a sense of personal relationship to him;

(2) such an understanding and appreciation of the personality, life, and teaching of *Jesus* as will lead to experience of him as Savior and Lord, loyalty to him and his cause, and will manifest itself in daily life and conduct;

(3) a progressive and continuous development of Christlike *character;*

(4) the ability and disposition to participate in and contribute constructively to the building of a *social order* throughout the world, embodying the ideal of the fatherhood of God and the brotherhood of man;

(5) the ability and disposition to participate in the organized society of Christians—the *church;*

(6) an appreciation of the meaning and importance of the Christian *family,* and the ability and disposition to participate in, and contribute constructively to, the life of this primary social group;

(7) a Christian interpretation of life and the universe; the ability to see in it God's purpose and plan; a *life philosophy* built on this interpretation;

(8) the assimilation of the best religious experience of the race, preeminently that recorded in the *Bible,* as effective guidance to present experience.[5]

An example of a denominational use of the essential ideas in this statement, with a regrouping of several items and a progressive application of each basic objective to the specific needs of junior and senior highs and of older youth, is included here (pages 44-48). Each of the items is elaborated in some detail in a statement (produced by the Board of Education and Publication, American Baptist Convention),

[5] *The Curriculum Guide for the Local Church.* Developed co-operatively by Protestant Evangelical Forces of the United States and Canada. Copyright, 1950. Used by permission. Committees of the National Council of Churches are now at work revising this document and developing objectives for age groups.

43

which serves as a basic document for curriculum building and for local church activity. Each local youth leader should make constant use of some such comprehensive statement as this, including aims formulated by his own denomination. The goals should be referred to frequently by young people in program building and in study-discussion sessions.

THROUGH CHRISTIAN EDUCATION WE SEEK TO GUIDE

A. JUNIOR HIGHS (INTERMEDIATES)

1. *In Relationship to God*
   (1) to know God as Creator, Sustainer, Ruler, and Heavenly Father
   (2) to develop a warm personal relationship with him, and to seek to do his will.

2. *In Relationship to Jesus Christ*
   (1) to an understanding and appreciation of the teachings, personality, life, death, and resurrection of Jesus;
   (2) to a growing commitment and loyalty to him as Savior and Lord which will manifest itself in daily life and conduct.

3. *In Relationship to the Bible*
   (1) to know and appreciate the Bible as the revelation of God to men in all ages;
   (2) to use the Bible effectively in their own Christian living.

4. *In Relationship to the Church*
   (1) to the desire and ability to participate as loyal members in the fellowship and work of the Christian church;
   (2) to an awareness of its heritage, its influence in history, its continuing mission and responsibility in the world.

5. *In Personal Christian Growth*
   (1) to grow in Christlike character;
   (2) to develop a sense of responsibility for conduct in every area of life.

6. *In Relationship to Others and to Society*
   (1) to live as Christians in the family and other group relationships including society at large;
   (2) to show Christian love and concern for all people.

WHITHER BOUND?

B. SENIOR HIGHS

1. *In Relationship to God*

(1) to an increasing awareness of the reality of God and a reverence for him;

(2) to a deeper understanding of God's revelation of himself in the universe, in the Bible, and supremely in Jesus Christ;

(3) to an increasing fellowship with God through prayer and worship; to an insight into the purposes of God, and their personal responsibility for the working out of those purposes;

(4) to the appropriation of the power of the Holy Spirit for the transformation and enrichment of life.

2. *In Relationship to Jesus Christ*

(1) to a knowledge of the life, teachings, death, and resurrection of Jesus Christ;

(2) to an appreciation of his unique person and character, his attitude toward men, and his revelation of God to men;

(3) to a deeper understanding of Jesus as the bearer of the good news of God's love for the world;

(4) to a definite personal commitment to Jesus Christ as Lord and Savior;

(5) to an increasing willingness to live as his disciples;

(6) to a wholehearted allegiance to him as the Way, the Truth, and the Life.

3. *In Relationship to the Bible*

(1) to a broader understanding of the Bible as a whole and its application to personal and social problems in our day;

(2) to a recognition of the value of the Bible for a proper understanding of the movements of God in history and the development of the Christian faith;

(3) to an increased appreciation of the unique message of the Word of God and its helpful guidance in right living;

(4) to a skillful, joyful, constant, and prayerful use of the Bible under the guidance of the Holy Spirit as interpreter.

4. *In Relationship to the Church*

    (1) to a deeper understanding of the nature and purpose of the Christian church;

    (2) to an appreciation of the church as a divine fellowship that is an expression of the Christian faith;

    (3) to an intelligent and active church membership, including participation in fellowship, study, worship, and service of the church;

    (4) to an enriched feeling of belonging to a world-wide Christian community;

    (5) to increased sharing in activities carried on by Christian churches working together.

5. *In Personal Christian Growth*—to stimulate the development of the qualities of Christian personality and character sufficient for all of life's situations, including:

    (1) an ability to think independently but with respect for the opinions of others;

    (2) a wholesome attitude in all relationships between young men and women;

    (3) a keen appreciation of Christian family life and a sense of individual responsibility for making a worthy contribution to a happy home life;

    (4) the development of qualities of leadership;

    (5) increasing ability to respond to the leadership of God's spirit in life;

    (6) an increasing sense of their responsibility as stewards of time, abilities, and money:

    (7) growing strength that comes from an honest practice of the Christian faith;

    (8) courage to carry on in the face of life's disappointments;

    (9) a firm belief that every Christian is called to serve God through his daily occupation and all other relationships.

6. *In Relationship to Others and to Society*

    (1) to the discovery and practice of a Christlike attitude toward, and a personal appreciation of, others;

(2) to a creation of a passion for freedom and for justice based upon Christ's teaching of love for all people;

(3) to a development of convictions that will enable them to act according to the Christian conscience in all community relationships;

(4) to the ability and the desire to share Christ with others;

(5) to the acceptance of the responsibility for making the greatest possible contribution to the building and extending of the kingdom of God through the missionary program of the church, with proper attention to the challenge of full-time Christian service.

C. OLDER YOUTH

1. *In Relationship to God*

(1) to achieve a maturing faith in God as maker and controller of the universe, as love, as one who can be fully trusted, as the source of true security, and as fully revealed in Jesus Christ;

(2) to recognize God as sovereign over the whole of life, and as one who takes a personal interest in all that they do.

2. *In Relationship to Jesus Christ*

(1) to gain a deeper understanding and appreciation of the life and teachings of Jesus Christ, the meaning of the resurrection, and the new life Christ has made available for all now and in the life everlasting;

(2) to discover the power in the living presence of Jesus Christ through the Holy Spirit.

3. *In Relationship to the Bible*

(1) to gain a more thorough understanding of biblical content and doctrine;

(2) to see that the Bible reveals the plans and purposes of God;

(3) to use the Bible as an indispensable help for daily living;

(4) to a new appreciation of the literature of the Bible.

4. *In Relationship to the Church*

(1) to give the church its rightful place in their lives;

(2) to help them discover valid reasons for regularity in church attendance;

(3) to find their place of responsibility in the church;

(4) to participate actively in winning others to Christ;

(5) to assume leadership in the local and larger Christian fellowship;

(6) to learn in sequence the story of the church through the ages;

(7) to see that the church's message is relevant to their lives.

5. *In Personal Christian Growth*

(1) to gain a better understanding of themselves, to achieve a greater degree of emotional maturity, and to develop in Christian character;

(2) to channel their desire to change conditions around them into making the world more Christian;

(3) to find their vocation in the light of what God wants them to do with their lives;

(4) to utilize opportunities for leadership development in church;

(5) to develop their personal devotional life through Bible study and prayer;

(6) to grow in awareness that all good gifts come from God, and that they are stewards of these gifts.

6. *In Relationship to Others and to Society*

(1) to reach a more mature conviction that members of all races are equal in God's love;

(2) to enlarge their friendships to include members of other races, other denominations, and other faiths, and to derive the richest possible experiences from them;

(3) to pattern their quest for a life partner after the ideals for a Christian home clearly set forth in the Bible and exemplified in the finest Christian homes they know;

(4) to work and pray for the fulfillment of Jesus' prayer, "Thy kingdom come; thy will be done, on earth as it is in heaven";

(5) to accept responsibility for seeking Christian solutions for community, political, economic, and international problems.

The emphases of the United Christian Youth Movement

How we got them. The five program areas, or emphases, of the Youth Fellowships have had a history. When the denominational Youth Fellowship organizations were first started, many of them secured the help of youth in listing and grouping the kinds of things in which Christian youth are concerned. Then they established goals, or emphases, and a pattern of committees or commissions to carry out these goals in the local church. Nationally, no two denominational patterns were identical. The significant fact, however, was not that there were some differences, but that there were so many similarities.

A comparative study of these patterns was undertaken. In a meeting of the denominational directors of youth work at Columbus, Ohio, where report was made of this study, the author pointed out that there was no fundamental reason for the differences, and proposed that common emphases be agreed upon. Later, at Otterbein College in 1949, the United Christian Youth Movement accepted a proposal of the Westminster Fellowship, looking toward the development of common emphases for general adoption by the denominations and by UCYM. This was a thrilling moment. In August, 1950, at St. Thomas, Ontario, the proposal for common commissions was adopted by a committee of young people and adult leaders. This proposal was approved more formally in September, 1951, and the five program areas became a reality. These have now become the basis of functioning of the UCYM and of most of the denominations.

Many churches now use these five areas as names for program commissions or committees. Denominations not formally committed to this pattern of commission organization still have them as a basis of comparison as they build their own program.

What the emphases include. The following is a broad outline of the areas of concern and the underlying purposes:

THE YOUTH FELLOWSHIP

small church (handwritten margin note)

1. CHRISTIAN FAITH

Purpose: to help youth grow in a vital Christian faith and life

Suggested areas of concern
Christian beliefs
Personal Christian commitment
Personal enrichment and growth
Bible study
Prayer
Worship
Yoke group experience
Personal conduct (Christian moral standards)
The Christian heritage
Meaning of church membership

2. CHRISTIAN WITNESS

Purpose: to help youth make known to others the way of Christ by all they say and do

Suggested areas of concern
Evangelism (personal and group)
Stewardship (time, talents, and material possessions)
Churchmanship (participation in the life of the local church)
Christian vocation (all vocations)

3. CHRISTIAN OUTREACH

Purpose: to help youth know and accept their responsibility in the world-wide mission of the church

Suggested areas of concern
Home missions
Foreign missions
The ecumenical movement
Interchurch aid (relief and reconstruction)
Peace and world order

4. CHRISTIAN CITIZENSHIP

Purpose: to help youth understand community needs and, on the basis of Christian convictions, work to meet these needs through personal influence and group action

Suggested areas of concern
Service to the local church

Service to the community
Intergroup relations
  interracial
  interfaith
  intercultural
Industrial relations
Economic problems
Social problems (alcohol, dope addiction, gambling, juvenile delinquency, etc.)

5. CHRISTIAN FELLOWSHIP

Purpose: to help youth experience in all their relationships the bond of Christian fellowship which comes from their common faith

Suggested areas of concern
Local church as a fellowship
Christian home life
Boy-girl relations
Recreation
Interchurch relations (denominational and interdenominational)
Leisure time
Creative arts
Service to members of the armed forces and conscientious objectors

How to use the emphases. These program areas may be put to work through worship themes, study-discussion topics, and action projects. There are different ways of organizing to do this:

1. Some groups have committees, or commissions, each with a chairman.

2. Others work all together for a period of time on each emphasis, without committees or commissions.

3. Still others use the emphases as a basis for balanced and comprehensive program planning for meetings, worship services, study sessions, and action projects, even though a different structure of committee organization is used.

The second plan is widely used in small churches. The third might apply, for example, to Disciples of Christ churches. (See Christian Youth Fellowship Handbook, *This Is CYF,* Christian Board of Publication.)

If a Fellowship does not wish to use a five-commission plan, it can use a three-commission plan by combining the areas on Christian Faith and Christian Witness, and the areas on Christian Outreach and Christian Citizenship.

It is assumed that there will also be a *cabinet* or *council* made up of the executive officers, commission chairmen and adult adviser (s), with such concerns as:

1. General program planning
2. Leadership training
3. Matters of general finance
4. Public relations
5. General correlation

POTENTIALITIES OF THE YOUTH FELLOWSHIP MOVEMENT

The possibilities which lie within the Youth Fellowship movement know almost no limit. For the first time in the history of the Christian religion, it is now possible to concentrate in the local church upon one all-inclusive youth organization and program whose aims are as broad as is the mission of the church itself. For the first time in the history of Protestantism, the scattered concepts of youth work and the differing terminologies are simplified and unified in the Youth Fellowship, with a common terminology and philosophy shared by most of the denominations.

In the local community this means that young people who attend the same school, work in the same factory or office, or live in the same neighborhood, can talk the same language and share the same ideas and materials. In very small communities they may even hold their meetings together regularly or for shorter periods, rotating, if desired, in the different churches. In larger communities they may hold coaching clinics, rallies, retreats, and training classes in which they exchange plans and build their programs along similar lines. Even more important than common terminology and ideas about youth work, they can present a united front for co-operative Christian action in the community.

Within the denominations, strong support for the national and world mission has already been achieved. There is greater understanding of the denominational heritage, and of the wide scope of work. Wider participation of youth in denominational plans and planning takes places. And now there are strong area and national youth-guided youth organizations.

For co-operative Protestantism, this means that young people may receive training in interdenominational co-operation at the grass-roots level in the local community. The ecumenical movement, if the right steps are taken, may turn to youth for adequate understanding and support in the future. Without youth to undergird it, no interdenominational movement can have a great future. Without the co-operation of the Christian forces represented in the different denominations, the Christian witness in the community and to the world is weak. The name given to the recognized channel for this co-operation is the *United Christian Youth Movement.*

In the Youth Fellowship movement, there is the enormous potential, the glorious hope, that God's will for our times, for evangelism and social justice, may be expressed with power and united voice through the medium of disciplined and dedicated youth. These youth must be bound together in a fellowship which crosses denominational, geographical, racial, and national lines, and acknowledges Jesus Christ as Lord.

CHAPTER III

THE MEETINGS

"Let us consider how to stir up one another to love and good works, not neglecting to meet together . . ." [1]

WHY HAVE MEETINGS?

Just before the big game, the entire student body meets in a rally. Before every big air operation, the officers assemble for briefing. Prior to any great decision, the board of directors or the stockholders meet. The business firm, the school faculty, the political party, the luncheon club, the grange or labor union, all must have their regular meetings.

So, also, the youth of the church need to meet. Without regular face-to-face meetings, there can be no true Youth Fellowship. And there is an extra reason for meeting as Christian youth — the very nature of the church demands it. For the church is unique in its mission and in the quality of its fellowship with one another and with God. Christianity says that each personality is of sacred worth in the sight of God. Democratic functioning is therefore important, with each individual responsible for thinking, planning, and working co-operatively. Through meetings of various types, the Fellowship is built, its vitality and usefulness enlarged.

Here are some of the results of various types of Youth Fellowship meetings: (1) plans are made; (2) spirit is generated; (3) ideas are exchanged; (4) loyalties are established; (5) knowledge and insight are shared; (6) group thinking occurs; (7) leadership abilities are developed; (8) personality

[1] Hebrews 10:24-25.

growth takes place; (9) business is transacted; (10) projects are completed; (11) good clean fun is enjoyed; (12) genuine worship is experienced; (13) the presence of God is felt; (14) the Christian community (or church) is established, strengthened, and enlarged.

Young people meet for *worship* — and by their fellowship in a common experience of the presence of God, their association is greatly enriched. They meet for *study* — and some adult, by sharing his broader experience and knowledge, makes possible the fellowship of learning. At other times they meet for *discussion* — and by each sharing his insights, all learn something new. Young people meet for *recreation* — and their common laughter and enjoyment of play make for personality growth in one another. Young people meet to *plan* and to *work* — and thus, becoming deeply committed to share in a common purpose, gain the satisfaction of achieving what they have set out to do in Christian service. Young people also share loyally in all the meetings of the church, contributing and benefiting from the wider fellowship which is characteristic of this divine institution.

Yes, *we need meetings* — good ones. We need clear purposes, vital content, effective procedures, tangible results. Here is the focal point for success in church work with youth. We need *discussion meetings that click, devotional meetings that inspire, business and planning sessions that really get results.* There is vitally important work to be done.

TIMES OF MEETINGS

The church's youth program includes meetings at various times on Sundays and weekdays. Each of these sessions should have a distinctive purpose as an accepted meeting of the Youth Fellowship. In most churches the weekly program includes two regular Youth Fellowship meetings on Sunday

— the Sunday morning session of the church school and the Sunday evening youth meeting. In many churches there are regular *meetings between Sundays* — sometimes weekly, sometimes monthly. Other churches have meetings at less regular intervals. Some churches with more than one age group do not find it possible to have two Sunday sessions weekly for each group — junior high, senior high, older youth — and are compelled to broaden the functions of the morning or the evening session, as the case may be, or to consolidate the two or three groups.

The Fellowship class and department—the Sunday morning church school session

The Sunday morning church school in many churches draws the greatest attendance of young people. Smaller churches may have but one class; larger churches may have separate departments and classes for each age group. Regardless of the number of classes and departments and of the presence or absence of separate rooms, the Sunday church school session of young people is a part of the Youth Fellowship. Each department is a *Fellowship* department, each class is a *Fellowship* class; for example, "the seventh-grade class of the Junior High Fellowship." Although classes break up the age-group Fellowships into study units, the Fellowship is still functioning through them. In an increasing number of churches, the young people have separate class and department rooms. This permits the use of the Youth Fellowship name and symbol, appropriate wall pictures, and specialized literature and equipment.

In churches which do not have separate class and department rooms, ways may sometimes be found to furnish reminders that the church school session is one of the meetings of the Fellowship, through posters, symbols, banners, and literature. Frequent announcements may be made of other activities of the Fellowship by Youth Fellowship officers.

Here is a typical time schedule for the Sunday morning session:

9:30 Fellowship departmental sessions
10:00 Fellowship class sessions
10:40 Informal Fellowship (announcements, introductions, etc.)
11:00 Church worship service (all ages)

The Fellowship departmental sessions are frequently used for short worship services carefully planned to have special meaning to youth and so as not to duplicate church worship. Sometimes these sessions or a portion of the time may be used for preparing to worship, learning a new hymn, rehearsing a ritual, or gaining insight about the forms and materials of worship. Some churches use these sessions for interpretation of topics and problems of a practical nature not otherwise included in the program — for example, getting acquainted with local church organization and leaders, missionary events and personalities, appreciation of religious music, art, and literature. Suggestions regarding this session will be found in Chapter VI on "The Fellowship at Worship."

Usually the Fellowship class sessions are used for the study of the Bible and related materials organized in a comprehensive curriculum. This curriculum, produced by competent specialists in the denominational editorial department in consultation with many local and national leaders, incorporates the best help which can be found in reaching the basic objectives of Christian education as discussed in the previous chapter. Usually the class discussion is led by the teacher, though often he will enlist the help of the junior or senior highs or older youth who are in his class. On occasion he will help them to prepare and teach the lesson themselves.

The Fellowship meeting—the Sunday evening session

The evening meeting has always had special appeal for young people. Perhaps this is, in part, because they have traditionally had more direct responsibility for planning and leading the session. They feel that it belongs to them in a special sense. Often this meeting is the heart of their loyalty and interest. Through this session, millions of adults now active in church and community life and millions of young people now active in the youth program have learned to pray, to speak in public, to plan and lead meetings.

The time schedule for the evening meeting varies according to local conditions and needs. Where there is a Sunday evening church service, the youth meetings may precede or follow.

A typical schedule, when the youth meetings *precede,* is:

6:15 Youth Fellowship meetings
7:30 Church service
8:30 "Social Half" (at the church) or "Fireside" (in a home)

A typical schedule, when the youth meetings *follow,* is:

7:00-8:00 Church service
8:00-9:00 Youth Fellowship meetings

Another schedule well suited to the needs of rural and city churches whose members live at some distance from the church is this:

5:15 Church service (vespers)
6:15 "Chupper" (light supper with fellowship features)
7:00 Youth Fellowship meetings
8:00 "Supersing" or "Firesides"

When no evening church service is held, the youth groups have more freedom in scheduling discussion meetings, audio-visuals, and social periods. Many churches conduct Sunday evening sessions with simultaneous groups for adults and children as well as youth, sometimes in a "College of Life" pattern with courses running for a series of weeks.

Junior high groups sometimes meet in the afternoon. In Canada and in some parts of the United States, the youth meetings in some churches are held on weekday evenings rather than Sunday, and are sometimes preceded or followed by social times, committee sessions, business meetings, or planning sessions. Leaders in at least one denomination have been encouraging a two- or three-hour weekday meeting for junior highs, with good results.

The type of program for the evening meetings varies widely. For the most part the meetings are somewhat more informal than the morning sessions in their study program, their discussion, and their program elements. Usually they provide for shorter units, or even for many single-session topics, on individual problems or themes.

Junior highs are at the age when they greatly need the experiences which cluster around this type of session. For one thing they need to spend more time with the church crowd, and to have more opportunity for the building of church-centered fellowship and loyalty. They are more crowd-minded than children. Being more self-sufficient, they are freer to choose a secular crowd in preference to the church group, or to reject the group experience for TV or other private activity. They need the enlarged insight to be gained from further thinking about Christian things. Also, they need very much at this stage in life the feeling of belonging, of sharing in group experience, and the training which the young people's meetings offer.

A crisis point arrives in the life of every individual as he steps over into early adolescence. Will the church be central or marginal in his life? Will the church youth group be his "gang," or some other? And more specifically, is he going to start at once to establish the pattern of attending regularly the Sunday evening meeting and becoming an accepted and active part of all Junior High Fellowship activity? Parents, teachers, and other adult leaders can do much to help achieve these significant goals.

Senior highs, in the evening meeting, find opportunity to express those ideas and abilities which are now coming increasingly into the center of their lives. They need many opportunities to express their thoughts; to try out their skills; to have the rough edges knocked off; to learn from their successes and failures; to develop confidence, poise, and effectiveness; to be a functioning part of a vital church group.

Older youth also need more time to develop their religious thinking and to improve their religious skills. Whether employed or students, their interests are broadening; their spiritual life is deepening. They need freedom to explore for themselves the vast range of religious thought and its application to the problems today. They need the checks and balances which come from comparing their own thinking with that of the great thinkers of the past and present, and with that of young people of their own age.

Two sessions on Sunday (morning and evening) seem exceedingly short to set over against many hours each week of university lectures or business training. Sometimes even irreligious indoctrination becomes a major part of these experiences. Still, much can be accomplished by using to the maximum the Sunday experiences to interpret and transform the activities and thoughts of the week. This is a large order, the Christianizing — evangelizing — of all areas of life, which makes the evening meeting, as well as the morning study class and regular church worship, imperative.

Those older youth who are compelled by local circumstances to meet with younger youth should be encouraged at two points: first, to enter fully into the discussion and devotional services with those who are younger, sharing their best thinking and mature leadership; and second, to find ways, through private reading and personal or group conversations among themselves and with their minister, adult adviser, and other respected leaders, to stimulate further thought and study.

Between Sundays

Fellowship meetings and events. Between Sundays the Youth Fellowship may have regular weekly meetings or special sessions on call as need arises. The weekly meetings may be of several types — a youth prayer meeting, a fellowship cell (or yoke) group, a Bible study class, a youth-night program, a business or planning session, recreation or service activity (such as hospital cheer groups). These activities may occur on a weekday evening, afternoons after school, on Saturday, or even in the early morning (a prayer group, for example). Some junior high groups hold their regular weekly meeting on a weekday afternoon or early evening. Many churches, rural and city, make a practice of declaring one night of the week as "Youth Night" and concentrating various activities and meetings on that night; some youth groups share in a "Church Night" when all ages are represented.

Special weekday meetings of many types are an established part of the program of most Youth Fellowships. These include banquets and other social events, dramatics, "song fests," business meetings, work projects, service activities, coaching clinics, interchurch leagues, conferences, rallies, and retreats. These must be timed on the monthly calendar so as to avoid unnecessary competition, and to fit into the schedules of the young people who are in the group. The test of whether a Youth Fellowship is really functioning lies in the use it makes of weekday opportunities to express the ideas discussed on Sunday in practical life, in group fellowship, and in service projects. These require between-Sunday meetings.

The Fellowship weekday club. Considerable difference of opinion exists concerning the place of weekday clubs in the Youth Fellowship program. Some leaders emphasize the fact that between-Sunday clubs have been, and continue to be, a large factor in the lives of many young people. These clubs, they say, have filled a real need, especially with early adolescents, millions of whom have been enrolled in Scout and Y groups, the 4-H, and other clubs. They emphasize hobbies, crafts, athletics, and individual achievements. They have had large appeal because of their cultivation of the feeling of progress and achievement, the wide scope and variety of their activity and interest units, and the effectiveness of their organization and leadership training. These clubs, mothered by the church, and committed to a strong religious emphasis, are many of them making use of church buildings for their meetings and of church members for their leaders.

Other leaders feel differently. They emphasize the need for simplicity and unity in the Youth Fellowship program and organization. They believe there is danger of divided loyalty and competitive interest. Some prefer to have all activities coeducational.

In recent years a trend has been growing in these club organizations toward closer association with the churches. An example is the "God and Country" award of the Boy Scouts of America, with stages of progress based upon the same five program areas used by the Youth Fellowship. Encouragement in this program is given by the Scout organization to local church-sponsored and church-controlled troops. Many Y organizations are committed to a policy of church-sponsored clubs which may be correlated with other aspects of the Youth Fellowship program. Under certain conditions it is quite possible and desirable to make such club programs an official part of the age-group Youth Fellowship program. In some churches weekday club units of the Youth Fellowship are being established with diversified interests and appeal. Some of these are coeducational.

In certain denominations the national program provides for Fellowship girls' guilds and boys' clubs as part of the Youth Fellowship activity in the local church. These clubs meet after school, on a weekday evening, or on Saturday.

TYPES OF MEETINGS

Every type of meeting which Christian youth in a church group could conceivably hold is included in the range of meetings of the Fellowship. The fact that the Fellowship meetings are classified does not mean that they are always distinct. Many meetings of the Fellowship combine elements such as worship and study, worship and expression, study and service, service and recreation, business and recreation.

Worship

One type of service which brings the Fellowship together frequently is *worship*. Young people need the experience of regular participation with adults in the worship services of the church. They also require graded experiences of worship planned to meet their own special needs, and to unify their fellowship and establish it on a truly religious basis.

Worship may be the major part of a meeting or it may be one phase of a meeting. Whenever and wherever Christian young people bind their hearts together in search of God, in adoration and praise of him, in sensing his presence, in listening to his voice and waiting upon his will, in commitment to Christ and to his purposes, there is worship. This worship may be short or long, formal or informal. It is quite usual to plan graded worship services in connection with the regular Sunday morning sessions, or a brief devotional period as part of the Sunday evening meeting.

Study classes

Another type of meeting which the Fellowship frequently has is in the form of *study classes*. A large proportion of the churches include such classes for youth as part of the Sunday church school session of the Fellowship. Study is not limited, however, to the church school hour, but takes place in various ways in the Sunday night meetings and in weekday classes.

Study certainly includes leadership training courses and mission units. The Bible, Christian teachings and doctrines, church history and biographies, the problems of personal and group living — these subjects and many more are considered in classes and meetings of the Fellowship.

Expressional activity

The Fellowship also meets at other times for *expressional activity*. This is the type of meeting which is commonly associated with the Sunday night meeting and with meetings of girls' or boys' clubs or coeducational groups during the week. Expressional meetings are varied: The young people may speak . . . sing and give musical programs or choric readings . . . produce plays and dramas . . . give readings . . . invite adult or youth outside speakers or performers.

Discussion

Many of the meetings of the expressional type are used for discussion. This type of session is also used largely in the church school class. Developments in the study of group dynamics have helped to make these discussions more vital. Religious problems of the members of the church, school, and community — any type of subject and problem which interests young people and which is of real concern to their spiritual welfare — may be the occasion for discussion.

Workshop or service activity

The *service* or *activity* or *workshop* meeting is another type of meeting in which the Fellowship engages. Some of the meetings are for planning, others for organizing materials, creating or beautifying objects, or engaging in activities requiring the development of skill or rehearsing — such as a verse-speaking choir or drama group.

Some churches have regular or special youth choirs, others have drama workshops. In some, there may be mimeographing to do, or poster making; a weekly or monthly news sheet for the young people; church mailing, or bulletins to handle. Or missionary projects, relief packages, clothing drives, white cross bandages and supplies. Or church beautification projects, paint-pot parties, "fix things up" parties. The full range of interests and skills, hobbies and creative activity, such as those incorporated in the program of the Scouts, the Y, 4-H clubs, the Camp Fire Girls, and other youth groups, may be included in the club program and weekday meetings of the Fellowship.

Social

Occasionally the Fellowship meets for *recreation* or *entertainment*. It may be once a quarter, once a month, or in some churches, once a week. A fireside in a home, or a fellowship period at the church, each Sunday night, offers a regular meeting time for youth in some churches. Groups within the

E   65

Fellowship, such as weekday clubs or interest groups, may also meet for social activities — hikes, snow parties, hay rides, etc.

Business

Another type of meeting is *business*. The whole Fellowship needs at least an annual business meeting to elect officers, to hear reports on the past year's work, and to plan for the new year. Most Fellowships meet periodically during the year for general business purposes. The cabinet and commissions, or committees, meet frequently (preferably once a month) to plan the work of the Fellowships — these are business or program-planning meetings. The trend of the times seems to be toward less formal business sessions and more emphasis upon creative planning through an annual retreat, quarterly check-up meetings, and monthly workshops.

ELEMENTS OF SUCCESS IN MAKING MEETINGS CLICK

Good meetings need imagination. They demand resourcefulness. And they justify the best efforts of all concerned. This is because so much hinges upon them. There is spirit to be generated, interest to be kindled, progress to be made in individual religious growth and group achievement. God must be brought near to youth. The Christian faith must become a driving force in their lives. Most of the purposes for which the Youth Fellowship exists depend largely upon meetings for their effectiveness. This being so, certain tested elements assure success. Here are some of them.

Variety

A very welcome feature in youth meetings is variety. Mere novelty is no substitute for quality of content and genuineness of spirit, but variety does help to create interest and to sustain attention. The Christian religion is an exciting force,

66

hence it is sacrilegious to make it seem dull and tame and uninteresting, especially with young people, who like surprises . . . the unusual. It is amazing what the fertile imaginations of young people can produce, and how much fun and satisfaction they get out of conducting meetings of an unusual nature. Caution should be exercised to avoid that which is inconsistent with Christian ideals, or variety which is mere stunts.

Inject variety into meetings in various ways — in room arrangements, decorations, worship centers; in unusual ways of doing the usual things with music, Scripture, prayer, discussion; in the type of meeting planned. Focal centers for worship or discussion may, for example, use many physical objects to create a setting for varied themes.

The Scripture may be presented through tableaux, pantomimes, dramatic sketches, tape or wire recorder, records; by antiphonal, dialogue, or narrative readers, or by verse-speaking choirs. Novelty and interest may be supplied through quiz programs, the use of telephone, radio, TV, recorders, slides, motion pictures, campfire programs (with imitation campfire), special day services (Youth Week, Race Relations, Brotherhood, Bible, UN Sundays, Mother's and Father's Days, Independence Day, Labor Sunday, World-wide Communion Sunday, Reformation Sunday, Christian Education Week). There may be symposiums, panels, forums, role-playing, and special ceremonials.

Unity

A good meeting creates a clear and orderly impression. This comes, first, from having a clear-cut aim, and then from a program built around a central theme related to this aim. All elements in the program — music, Scripture, prayer, discussion, presentation — should contribute something distinctive toward this aim. A valuable experience for young people to have is training in building programs in which all the elements have unity, and a strong, cumulative effect is achieved. Many good meetings with careful planning and a single objective reach a real climax as the discussion progresses and as plans are made to follow through with some form of tangible action or service.

Real advantage comes from using the prepared denominational program materials or some adequate substitute. Such helps are carefully planned to achieve a unified effect and to deal with a definite aim. This aim takes into consideration the materials produced for other sessions of the Fellowship in which the same young people are participating. It is a good idea to consult the table of contents of hymnbooks and poetry collections for their topical classification. Scripture passages may be located readily in concordances.

Appeal

An effective meeting has both surface appeal and depth appeal. To attract young people, the meeting must quickly excite attention. It must sound and look interesting, i. e., it must have surface appeal. However, if a meeting is to hold young people and produce outcomes in action, it must have what may be called "depth appeal." This means that it must produce response of the emotions, the will, and the mind, as well as of the curiosity. Sometimes this response may be assisted by the wording of the theme itself, so that it starts thought, and suggests the deeper level on which the meeting program will move. For example, the theme, "Are You Marriageable?" was used by a Christian college professor for separate meetings of the Older Youth Fellowship and Young Adult Fellowship (single young adults) in the author's church. The theme attracted personal curiosity when announced, and also determined the level of discussions on the factors which make for success in building Christian home life. Similar results were attained through using the theme, "What's Your Answer?" for a series of four weekly meetings: "The Problem of Making the Right Decision," "Conflicting Loyalties," "Hollow Men," "The Problem of Dogma."

The choice of the plans and the ideas which go into the program also determine appeal. These plans and ideas must be attractively presented, and of vital concern to the life of youth today. The appeal of the meeting is also determined by the spirit in which it is conducted — the feeling of acceptance, of "belonging" on the part of each young person attending, the respect shown for his ideas, and the genuine enthusiasm revealed for Christian ideals. Discussion meetings must have what Dr. Haiman calls "emotional involvement" [2] if they are to strike deeply enough to maintain interest and to change attitudes and conduct. But there are ways of releasing tension through humor. Bitterness and withdrawal behavior may be avoided by creating a feeling of Christian friendliness and redemptive love.

Participation

A successful meeting produces active participation. Youth must become involved intellectually, emotionally, and practically, if they are to be interested, and if they are to learn, grow in ability to express themselves, and develop leadership skills. "This is a basic principle in young people's work: *Those who carry out or conduct the program should have a part in its creation.* We now know that better results can be achieved when the program is constructed co-operatively and in a democratic spirit. . . . The meeting, generally speaking,

[2] *Group Leadership and Democratic Action,* by Franklyn S. Haiman. Houghton Mifflin Company, 1951.

will be successful in direct proportion to the number of persons participating in the program in a meaningful way." [3] This participation may be through publicity, room arrangements, assigned parts in the meetings, or in informal, spontaneous discussion.

GROUP DYNAMICS IN YOUTH MEETINGS

"What makes a group tick?" asks a leader. "Why do some groups have more spirit than others? More stimulating meetings, more lively participation by all the members, fewer 'deadheads,' more energetic teamwork on action projects?"

"Group dynamics" is the name given to the study of such questions as these. Such study is helpful as a key to understanding effective ways of group thinking and planning which express the Christian spirit. The term is now widely used to refer to the psychological forces which stimulate the democratic functioning of groups. By "group" is meant a company of people who gather for educational or political purposes or for business planning. The Youth Fellowship meeting is such a group. It has the added factor of Christian love.

Group dynamics are helpful to youth meetings in a number of ways. Group discussion is one of the techniques of group dynamics when it is conducted along sound psychological and democratic lines. Developments in recent years have tended to make discussion procedures more vital, or dynamic. These developments include panels, group interviews, dialogues, "round tables," the question box, and symposiums.

One of these new approaches is the "buzz session." This involves dividing the group, when a problem arises in discussion, into small groups meeting simultaneously, usually in the same room, for six to ten minutes. Each person in turn

[3] From *The Young People's Meeting*, by Richard Hoiland. Copyright, 1935, The Judson Press. Used by permission.

expresses his ideas, and then each group reports its findings. This device stimulates full participation and free discussion.

Another useful approach is through "role-playing." This means that a problem situation of special value to the group is acted out spontaneously by individuals chosen from the group to play the roles as they think the individuals would react. The entire group then has opportunity to comment on the role-playing, and upon the problem raised and solutions offered. "Role-playing is acting out a situation to inform, persuade, or create a deeper understanding in the group involved. The members themselves play the parts, occasionally with a rehearsal and a few props, more often using only their imaginations to direct them." [4]

Here's the way it works. Suppose young people are discussing "The Importance of the Christian Church." The question arises, "How can we interest our friends in the Youth Fellowship meetings?" Someone suggests, "Let's role-play a visit to a home. Suppose there are two young people — a brother and a sister — neither of them interested. How would we handle the situation?" Two young people are chosen to act the parts of callers, and two to take the parts of the brother and sister. The role-players, after a brief conference to determine their plans, begin with the callers knocking on the door and being invited in. They tell about the church and its Youth Fellowship activities. Objections, misconceptions, and excuses are voiced by the brother and sister. These are discussed and finally a promise is made to attend next Sunday. Perhaps the parts are then reassigned, and the situation re-enacted, with different young people playing the roles. Thus, all become involved psychologically. Attitudes change, new insight is received.

[4] From *New Ways to Better Meetings*, by Bert and Frances Strauss. Copyright, 1951, by the Viking Press. Used by permission.

CHAPTER IV

THE PLANNING PROCESS

"All things should be done decently and in order." [1]

WHY IT'S NECESSARY TO PLAN

It doesn't happen by accident

A good lesson to learn early in life is that slipshod procedures produce meager results. Any attempt to whip up a cake, or for that matter to whip up a party or a meeting, without a reasonable amount of consideration of the ingredients and how to put them together successfully is likely to be doomed to failure.

The president of a Youth Fellowship in a small town, who was also quarterback on the football team, learned this the hard way. "Guess I am to blame for that Christmas party at the church being such a flop," he said. "I knew we had to plan our football plays at school, and practice to be sure each man knew what he was to do on each play. But I thought we could get by for the party without any real planning. Now I know it doesn't work that way."

Planning gets results

Honest effort invested in planning youth work usually pays off well. Among the hundreds of youth groups visited by the author in many different states, some stand out, invariably because good planning has been done. One such, in a medium-sized city, has a long series of achievements to its credit and has produced young people of superior leadership

[1] 1 Corinthians 14:40.

ability far out of proportion to its size — largely due to a sustained emphasis year after year on planning.

Are the parties getting dull, the meetings monotonous? Imaginative planning is a large share of the answer. Are a few doing all the work, and the others going along just for the ride? Plans which enlist all in a variety of interesting projects should make a difference. Is the group weak on worship and on devotional commitment? Do they lack in knowledge of the Bible and of the Christian faith? Is very little being done to reach others? The answer to each problem starts with a plan. Perhaps it is a six-week study emphasis on worship, or a series of youth worship services based on material from the *International Journal of Religious Education*. Or it may be a special Bible study group, an emphasis upon a Bible study unit in the regular denominational lesson materials for youth. Or it may be a "New Friends for Christ" visitation weekend — including Friday, Saturday and Sunday calling with invitations to the Sunday meetings and to a Saturday night social event. For almost every problem, a plan will help to solve it if we dedicate ourselves to the task of discovering and applying it.

That's how youth learns

There is a double reason why planning is important for youth. Not only does it produce visible results in the program; it also produces visible growth in those who do the planning. They learn how to plan. They mature in their resourcefulness, their dependability, their commitment to the Christian enterprise, their Christian character. And after all, that is what the church's youth program is primarily for — to produce *Christian personalities*. In this sense the *process* of planning is valuable in itself, even if nothing more should be accomplished. Yet this result is always a by-product of sincere effort for a worth-while purpose. The mistake should never be made of treating the process of planning as an end instead of as a means.

CLUES TO A SUCCESSFUL FELLOWSHIP

1. The secret of success is in good plans well executed.

2. Good planning involves good timing—start early, check up regularly, follow through.

3. Everyone pitches in better when everyone has helped plan.

4. Distribute the load by clear-cut assignments if you want to get good results.

5. The annual calendar of dates and emphases is the key to a balanced program.

WHEN SHOULD THE PLANNING BE DONE?

The annual retreat: . . . sets up the year's calendar

In this case the kind of "retreat" we are talking about is really a preparation for an advance — a withdrawal in order to get set to attack with courageous spirit and with well-worked-out strategy. More and more youth groups have been discovering that such retreats, held annually, are indispensable for program planning, spiritual strength, and morale building. "We can't get along without it," said the adult adviser of a very successful youth group. "That's where we have the fun of laying out our entire year's work — parties, meetings, projects, everything."

The *goals* of the retreat may be several. For example, here are a few representative voicings of aims as expressed in an area conference of local church youth officers: (1) "to develop a comprehensive calendar of events and emphases for the next twelve months"; (2) "to select a few main-track emphases and to formulate suggestions for reaching them — to be given detailed study by the cabinet at a later date"; (3) "to build a sense of group solidarity as the result of playing and working and worshiping together in an unusual setting"; (4) "to achieve a new understanding of our real task and a fresh sense of commitment to it."

The "quarterly check-up": . . . reviews progress

The secret of effective functioning is a periodic check-up to see if the plans — and the workers — are working. Once in three months is about right for a meeting of a "program council" made up of the officers, commission chairmen, and adult adviser. The calendar of events and emphases for the next three months should be examined in detail, and assignments made. A brief review of the past three months is in order to see if there is incomplete work. If changes need to be made, there is time to make adjustment. If new plans are to be added, this is the time to do it. Publicity should be carefully considered, and budgeted if money will be needed. New members may be assigned to commissions or to special committees or projects.

The monthly program planning meeting: . . . gets the work done

Many youth groups have learned the basic importance of monthly planning sessions. Here is where the work really gets done. Usually the Youth Fellowship cabinet meets monthly to dispose of official business and to plan details for the month ahead. In churches with separate age groups — junior highs, senior highs, and older youth — each cabinet needs to meet to initiate and co-ordinate plans, to assign responsibilities, and to check up on progress.

In Youth Fellowships of average size, or larger, there is also an important place for monthly planning sessions of the standing commissions or committees; i. e., Faith, Witness, Outreach, Citizenship, Fellowship, or the equivalent working groups by whatever names they are called. Such sessions may be for two distinct purposes: (1) planning the special events, projects, or emphases assigned to the particular commission; (2) planning the weekly meeting, or meetings, assigned to the commission which occur during the month. To be specific — the Fellowship commission, during the month of November, may plan the details of a December Christmas party, arrange for Christmas caroling, and, in addition, take direct responsibility for a Sunday evening youth meeting and a Sunday morning Youth Fellowship worship service at the church school hour.

Junior High Fellowships usually create short-term committees instead of appointing standing commissions. "In our planning meetings," said one junior high adviser, "I usually try to have most of the materials right at hand ready for use. They're quite good at filling in the details if I can get them started with a definite suggestion. We use the denominational materials, and they are very helpful."

A coaching clinic: . . . is a good idea

Once a year, or even more often, a planning session of a somewhat different nature is desirable — namely, the coaching clinic. The idea back of this session is to provide an opportunity for informal briefing and training; for example, of the new officers, when elected. Use may be made of denominational manuals, audio-visuals, chalk boards, diagrams, "Know Your Job" quizzes, and similar devices, to assist in the coaching process. The clinic feature may be supplied by dealing with specific "ailments" of the Youth Fellowship which need to be analyzed and "cured" by prescribing some quite definite remedies.

A special workshop now and then: . . . is a great help

The workshop spirit and approach are of great assistance to the planning process. If the group is planning a party, it should have on hand one or more good "idea books" for games and party features; also, materials for making decorations, place cards, invitations, and equipment needed for certain games.

A discussion meeting, if arranged, will require paper and pencils, Bibles and a concordance, discussion sources, and other reference materials. For a worship service, there should be hymnbooks and such resources as poetry, stories, pictures, compilations of worship materials and other aids.

Leadership training classes: . . . assist long-range planning

The Leadership Education Curriculum of the National Council of Churches, as used co-operatively by most of the denominations, provides many training courses for young people themselves and for their adult leaders. Such courses have great merit. They encourage long-range planning on a sound basis. They permit the exchange of good ideas and experience. They use approved textbooks and manuals which assemble the judgment and tested experiences of many people in different situations. Each youth officer and adult leader should be encouraged to take courses.

WHO DOES THE PLANNING?

The role of the leader

There is a definite place for the adult leader in the planning process. But it is not to make all the decisions, or even to think up all the ideas. The leader shares his experience in what has already worked, and what has not. He supplies judgment as to how much it is possible to achieve in a given time, and what are desirable and undesirable things to include in the program (factors of major importance to junior highs). He is aware of many ideas and plans from which to make choices. He can help by getting the planning process started early enough, in seeing that it is completed, in knowing when to hold back and when to add an idea or suggestion, or raise a question. His approach may be, "Would you like to try this?" "Do you think the program is strong enough at this point?" "Let's see now, how many projects have we lined up already for October?" "Have you noticed the ideas on this subject in this manual?"

Teachers and counselors — special assignments. Even if the teacher does not also serve as the Fellowship adviser, he may be able to help in the planning process by giving general encouragement and assistance in his teaching and personal counseling. Good ideas for service projects, and the desire to see them through, often come out of the class sessions; close co-ordination of the Sunday morning study program with other phases of the Youth Fellowship activity is essential. It is also quite usual for each teacher or other general counselor to take a special assignment to work with one of the Youth Fellowship commissions, to assist in planning the worship programs for the morning session, or to help with the parties or other special events.

The Youth Fellowship adviser. Many different ways of organizing and planning may be worked out within the Fellowship pattern. One of the best of these is to have one counselor (or a married couple) for each age-group Fellowship who is recognized as the Youth Fellowship adviser (or counselor, as he is called in some groups), with full responsibility for working with the young people in planning and carrying through the entire Fellowship program in the various Sunday sessions and weekday meetings. This adviser should meet regularly with the youth cabinet in the planning sessions and should maintain close relationships with the church board of Christian education and with the other adult leaders of youth.

The role of youth

How can everyone have a part in planning? As we have already seen, it is desirable for all the young people to share in the planning process, and it is possible for them to participate in an annual planning retreat. They may also be involved in committee or commission activities and planning, and be given specific responsibility from time to time for planning various parts of meetings, service projects, and social events. Junior highs, as well as older youth, are often eager to take such responsibility. It is quite feasible, every now and then, to use part of the Sunday morning or evening meeting for a brief planning session in which all participate, or to get quick reactions to alternate plans.

The officers and how they proceed. Here is one example of how the planning process worked in one church in a western state. The event was a Fall Kickoff Banquet. The broad outlines of the program were agreed upon at the annual retreat. The monthly program planning meeting decided upon the definite plans — speakers, theme, special music, and other features. The officers involved went to work on planning the details. The participants were approached. The invitations were designed and mimeographed, the decorations were planned, the time schedule was worked out in detail, and specific assignments were made for all responsibilities. The president and other officers shared in the planning, and assisted in checking up on plans. Thus a significant event took place with a feeling of satisfaction that it had been democratically planned and had been efficiently carried through.

The Youth Council. Churches that have two or more age-group Fellowships need an intergroup planning committee for the youth division of the church. This committee is often called the Youth Council. It plans for intergroup events, projects, and emphases, represents the young people in church-wide planning sessions, and assists in co-ordinating the age-group programs so as to avoid competing events.

The age-group cabinets. Each age-group Fellowship needs a group of officers who compose a cabinet. This group of youth leaders has a large responsibility for planning the week-by-week and month-by-month program, usually in a monthly cabinet meeting. The junior high cabinet is usually flexible and changeable in personnel, since the interest span of this age group is often quite short. The cabinet hears reports and recommendations of the officers, reviews suggestions of the adult leaders and young people, and delegates back to the officers and committees responsibility for action.

Regular committees or commissions. One point at which considerable variation occurs among denominations and in different local churches is that of committee or commission groupings and planning. The most typical plan now in operation involves a commission or committee for each of the five program areas — Faith, Witness, Outreach, Citizenship, Fellowship. Many junior high groups, because of the short span of interest, do not maintain standing committees. Many small churches do not have commissions; instead they work together on each area in turn. Many Student Fellowships use standing committees selected to meet local needs, or, dispensing with standing committees entirely, create special committees as need arises. Where committees exist, they have a job to do, and are an important link in the planning process. They should meet regularly and organize their task well. If they all do so, a surprising amount can be accomplished in a year.

Special committees. Such committees — created when a particular need arises, and released when the job is done — often have important work to do. The junior highs in one church, for example, decided to send handmade Sunday school notebooks and other supplies to a former junior high department member — a college graduate on a special mission to Japan. A committee was created, and plans were made for assembling the materials, putting them together, packaging them, and shipping them. "The gang" worked like mad, but had lots of fun, according to their own account. "We got a great thrill when we received back a package from Japan which included pictures which the children had painted, carp (fish) banners, and a huge appreciation roll with names signed in Japanese."

HOW PLANNING GETS DONE

Using a retreat effectively

The *place* of retreat is important. Whether in the mountains, at the beach, by a lake or a stream, in the woods, in a cabin, a resort hotel, a school dorm, a farmhouse, a private home, or just some favorite spot in your own or a neighboring church — there is advantage in withdrawing for prayer, fellowship, and creative planning, free from distractions.

The *time* of the retreat is likewise significant. It should be set at a date which will permit advance planning, and which fits into the plans of the members. In the author's own church, the youth officers take office early in May, and the Youth Council retreat is usually held in May or early June. Many churches use Labor Day or some other date in September. Others use Christmas vacation or New Year's Day or Easter week, Memorial Day, or midsummer. Sometimes a weekend is required, or Friday night and all day Saturday. Or a one-day retreat on a Saturday or a Sunday may suffice.

Much attention should be given to the detailed *time schedule,* to the *topics* or *problems* to be discussed, and to the *method* of conducting the retreat. The retreat itself should be planned with considerable care, and, ideally, with imagination. This is so that the entire group will plunge into the planning process with interest, with a clear sense of what is to be done, and with a spirit of eagerness to pool insights and judgments in accomplishing the most. The time schedule may provide for such items as the following:

(1) *Devotional moments*—morning watch, vespers, inspirational messages, closing dedication
(2) *Statement of purpose*—What do we hope to accomplish?
(3) *Discovery groups* (planning committees)
(4) *Reports and discussion*

Such a time schedule assumes a process of group participation with areas assigned to two or more small committees for exploration, report, and opportunity for free discussion. Keep in mind that a retreat is a freer and more creative type of session than a formal business session.

Some thought needs to be given to the question of *who* will attend. There are several possible answers. This retreat may be (1) for *all* young people of the church — junior high to college age; or (2) limited to those of an individual age group — junior high, senior high, or older youth; or (3) limited to the Youth Fellowship officers, committee or commission members, and adult advisers. The important thing is to include all those who are needed to do a thorough job — whichever plan is decided upon.

Building the annual calendar

The annual calendar is one of the most useful devices ever developed to assure comprehensive, long-range planning and effective week-by-week execution. The calendar is usually organized by months, and such items as the following are listed in parallel columns: (1) *date* (day, week, or longer, if required); (2) *event* or *emphasis* (for example, "Youth Week" or "visitation program"); (3) *intended for* ("cabinet" or "everyone"); (4) *details* ("bring lunch," "bring guests," "wear costume"). If desired, the regular Sunday meetings and other weekly events may be listed as well as the monthly committee meetings. Seasonal dates may be recorded, such as Thanksgiving, Christmas, New Year's Day, Easter, etc.

Many groups with regular commissions or committees start the process of building the calendar by assigning mimeographed forms to each commission with instructions to list their proposed projects, events, and emphases. The cabinet is instructed to list events and emphases of general significance not covered by the commissions. These proposals are assembled by the cabinet, which is responsible for building the master calendar, for co-ordinating the events and emphases, and for offering suggestions to avoid too much or too little activity at any one time or by any one commission. The calendar, when approved, may be transferred from the work sheets to a large printed wall calendar or poster.

Conducting a committee meeting

A committee meeting differs from a formal business session. It calls for a different technique. Formal rules of procedure for reaching decisions may not be required unless there is marked disagreement and, even then, only as a means of quick, clear, and fair action. It is important for all to share in discussion and planning, so that no one monopolizes the thinking, or dominates the group. Motions and voting help everyone to be clear about what is decided and to have a voice in it, and they also help a group to come quickly to a decision. Often, in informal committee meetings the chairman may say, "If there is no objection, by common consent we will consider it decided that . . ." or "We have discussed this matter long enough to discover that there are two points of view. Suppose we settle it by a straw vote." If formal vote is required, business procedures may be simplified, provided there is no objection. All involved in Youth Fellowship committee meetings should feel concerned that the spirit of Christian love and understanding be revealed, and that agreement always be reached by a democratic and truly Christian process.

Avoid getting bogged down in details. The classic comment about committees is that "they keep minutes and waste hours." This is because they follow detours from the main issues, and get bogged down in details. How can this be prevented? The chairman must do his part, likewise each member of the committee. The chairman's job is to keep the discussion moving and on the topic, and to help the group to point up alternate opinions or choices, together with the advantages and disadvantages in each. He should make sure that all share in the discussion without domination by anyone, including himself, and come quickly to a decision. He may need to help bring the discussion back to the main theme (by such comments as, "Are we getting off the subject?" or "Is this on the main issue?"). He may assist in reaching decision (by such comments as, "Have we reached agreement?" or "Are we ready for a vote?"). The job of the members is to help the chairman get things done, and done well. Each member can do so by making his comments concise and on the subject, by avoiding needless arguments, by listening when others talk, by suggesting specific action.

Make clear assignments. Issues or projects are not always ready for action when they are first raised. To someone must be assigned the job of thinking them through, and of formulating a definite proposal to be voted on at the next meeting. Other projects, though agreed upon, need to be referred to an individual or a subcommittee for further planning and the carrying out of details. It is important, in either case, that the assignments be clear — to the chairman, to the persons involved, and to the other members of the committee. This means a definite understanding of what is to be done, and when, and as to the amount of authority granted — is it power to act, or must the proposal be brought back to the committee for approval?

Check up on progress. Many projects and emphases are of such a nature that they are in the planning or the executing stages for a long time. A good chairman will call for frequent "progress reports." Some committees follow a plan on major projects of setting up deadlines when various phases are to be completed, and of calling for progress reports. Further planning sometimes may be necessary, or even a complete change in plans.

EVALUATION AND REPORT

An eye on the long-range goals

Most youth groups are nearsighted. Being so close up to what they are doing, they need the perspective of long-range goals and regular times for evaluating progress. The annual report to the local church and to the regional and national denominational offices is such an occasion; also, the annual retreat. Leadership training classes offer a similar opportunity, especially if conducted on an interchurch basis in the local community, at a camp, or at some other regional conference. Forms for appraisal may be developed locally, or secured from outside sources.

Don't try too much—or too little

Some young people are too ambitious, or perhaps too visionary; others are lacking in desire, or in imagination. A middle point should be found. "How much did we do last year, and how much more can we tackle this?" . . . "What are others doing? Why can't we?" . . . "Remember what happened at Christmastime last year, when we had to give up our plans because we had too much on?" Most groups doubtless should be prodded or encouraged into doing much more in practical service to express their Christian life.

When you fail—find out why and try again

One great advantage about youth work is the possibility of learning from a mistake before it is too late to do something about it. Temporary failure may often be used to produce ultimate success. It is important to find out *why* we failed. Was it because we didn't plan well or far enough ahead, because we didn't try hard enough, because we failed to use enough ingenuity, or lacked team spirit? Was it because we met with obstacles (which could have been overcome), because our interest sagged, or because the idea wasn't a good one in the first place?

When you succeed, make something of it

There is great psychological value when young people are able to recognize and measure success in the religious field, and when they gain the satisfactions and incentives for further endeavors which come from real good accomplished. The more superficial evidence — such as numbers, applause, physical articles produced, gifts made, money raised, programs presented — is important and should be publicized and given appropriate emphasis. But more important are the less tangible achievements, such as change of attitude, a new spirit of fellowship, individual growth in character. The skillful leader — adult or youth — will find means of expanding these spiritual achievements by highlighting them in conversations, announcements, worship, and prayer.

What kind of Christian personalities are you producing?

Again, the real measure of progress in youth work is not statistical, it is spiritual. What is happening to George, Ed, Jane, Sarah, and Alice? Are Christlike followers of Jesus being produced who are learning how to think and feel and act as he did? Are life choices — of vocation, of mate, of attitudes toward money and people — being made, and acted upon, in accord with his spirit and in harmony with the will of God? Are leadership traits and skills being developed and expressed in the group relationships and activities?

What's really happening in your church and community?

The acid test of the worth of the planning process, and of the reality of transforming experiences of individuals, is what is happening in the church as a whole and in the community. How much of a factor is the Youth Fellowship among adults and children in the church? What loyalties are being made evident, what service is being undertaken? What is taking place in the junior or senior high school, in the college, or in business life? Are Christian youth setting the standards, or are others doing so? Are others being influenced and attracted to the church? Are moral, social, economic, and political situations in the community being improved? There is evidence that individual Christianity is not becoming ingrown, and that the youth group is becoming a Christian force for good. The planning process and the activities that follow are abundantly worth while.

And some bring forth a hundredfold.

CHAPTER V

THE STRUCTURE

"The whole body, joined and knit together by every joint . . . , when each part is working properly, makes bodily growth and upbuilds itself in love." [1]

WHY ORGANIZATION IS ESSENTIAL

Not an end but a means

Organization, sometimes, is like the whistle on Mark Twain's Mississippi steamboat — which took so much steam to make it blow that the boat itself had to stop to build up pressure again before it could make any headway. A Youth Fellowship should be judged, not by the amount of organization or even by the amount of activity, but by the extent of its progress. If nothing much happens to change people and circumstances, then nothing much is accomplished, no matter how elaborate the structure or how smoothly it functions.

Without leadership there is confusion

There is a great difference between a mob and an army, a theater audience and a football squad, a free-for-all argument in a city park and a well-planned Youth Fellowship meeting or party. The difference is organization, which depends upon leadership. Even for a good discussion, there must be organization — a few guiding principles, a central theme or common ground of interest, a recognized leader or in a round table or a panel, a passing of leadership back and forth. To build a house, to run a school or a business, to carry through significant Youth Fellowship service projects, organization and leadership are essential.

[1] Ephesians 4:16.

Sound structure multiplies effectiveness

Good organization is important. Though no amount of organization can create spiritual power, good organization can diffuse it. We see this in the early Christian church. Jesus gathered a small group of young men and women around him and organized them into a band of disciples. He selected the twelve; he assigned responsibilities to them; he named a treasurer. He sent the twelve out two by two with specific instructions, and held sessions for report, coaching, and training, when they returned. He enlarged the organization. First there were twelve, then seventy, then five hundred; finally, a dynamic movement which changed the course of history.

To be sure, organization in itself has never made Christianity a vital force. Its power has come from above, often in spite of the structure. Nevertheless, the Christian movement has been given added strength by sound organization, and has always needed the church as an organized vehicle for its expression.

Protestant churches have learned what American history has confirmed: Democracy, though often slow in getting started, is in the long run actually more efficient. *No greater need exists in our time than an organized Christian youth movement which will combine dynamic spiritual power with sound structure and find expression in a vital program within the Christian church and beyond.*

SOME PRINCIPLES OF SOUND YOUTH ORGANIZATION

A living organism

The best type of simple organization we know is a living cell with capacity to grow, expand, adapt, perform functions, and even to reproduce itself. In a spiritual sense a good organization resembles an organism in that it has life and a reason for existence. This is especially true of a good Christian youth organization. A Youth Fellowship is like a living, growing cell.

Paul referred to the church as "the body of Christ." "For just as the body is one and has many members, and all the members of the body, though many, are one body, so it is with Christ. . . . Now you are the body of Christ and individually members of it" (1 Cor. 12:12, 27).

Simplicity—a word to small and large groups

Other things being equal, the simpler an organization is, the better. Many churches do not need an elaborate Youth Fellowship organization. One Youth Fellowship to cover the entire age range of twelve to twenty-five may be sufficient, or there may be place for two: for example, a junior high group of eight or ten members, and a combined senior high and older youth group of six or eight. Some churches have started and successfully maintained Youth Fellowships limited to five members. It is not necessary that the program and spirit be weak even though the numbers are few. As has been said, "The less there is of you, the more need to make the most of what there *is* of you." The offices and the committee functions can be combined. Some groups that are small in numbers prefer to assign each member to an office or committee task so as to enlist the fullest participation and provide for the fullest opportunity for training.

The principle of simplicity applies likewise to average-size groups and to large organizations of youth. Nothing is gained by creating wheels within wheels simply to expand organization. The more complex an organization becomes, the more inefficient it is likely to be, and, conversely, the simpler the structure, other things being equal, the more effective the results. A large Fellowship of youth may be organized along simple lines, with many tasks to be performed, and each person understanding clearly his relationship to the whole.

Comprehensiveness—unity

A sound principle of effective functioning is to include in one structure all the tasks for which a group of individuals are responsible and which are related to a common purpose, rather than to create separate organizations for each of the tasks. In this way unity and strength are attained.

Flexibility

A good organization needs to have sufficient flexibility to be able to adapt itself to differing circumstances and needs. The Youth Fellowship has shown itself to have this adaptability. It has demonstrated ability to serve the needs of churches large and small, city and rural, old and new, in many different types of community. It has worked well with employed youth and with students, sometimes with widely different patterns of organization and functioning, and with senior and junior highs. It has adapted itself well to communities without junior high schools, and to those with two-year or three-year junior high schools.

Democratic functioning

Democratic functioning is sound for a Christian youth organization for several reasons. It is *more Christian* in that it shows respect for each individual, and is fair in abiding by the will of the majority after full consideration of various points of view. It is *well grounded educationally* in that all who participate learn from the process, the mistakes as well as the successes. In the long run, it is *more efficient* because of the improvement which comes from co-operative planning, and because of the higher degree of commitment, under-standing, and enthusiasm.

Spiritual vitality

A Christian youth organization, if true to its essential nature, possesses the spark of divine energy which comes from God and which helps to make it unique. Its enthusiasm cuts deeper than mere pep or superficial physical excitement. Rightly conceived, such a strong sense of purpose underlies all that the Youth Fellowship does that it causes everyone to launch forth with initiative on old and new enterprises, to attract support through radiant faith, and to maintain per-sistent effort until the mission is accomplished.

THE YOUTH OFFICERS

General officers

The *president* should be a sincere Christian, active in the life of the church, well versed in the youth program, able to take the initiative, and capable of enlisting others in the program. He must be responsible for seeing that the whole program of the Fellowship is promoted, and that all sessions and meetings are well planned and conducted. This does not mean that the president will do everything himself, or that he will personally preside at all meetings. He must work with the cabinet and the adult leaders in planning the pro-gram of activities and meetings, and in frequent check-ups on functions and plans. His specific duties may include, for example: (1) presiding over business meetings of the Fellow-ship; (2) organizing the work of the cabinet and presiding over its meetings; (3) counseling with regular commission or committee chairmen, and appointing special committees; (4) helping adult advisers to relate the Fellowship activities to the entire church program.

The *vice-president,* ideally, should have qualifications similar to those of the president. In the absence of the president, he serves in that capacity. He may also be assigned a fixed responsibility — chairman, for example, of the program committee, made up of the commission chairmen and responsible for general planning of meeting programs — or he may have special responsibilities, as the cabinet may decide.

The *secretary* should be neat, orderly, efficient, and dependable. Duties may include: (1) keeping minutes of all business meetings; (2) sending notices of cabinet meetings; (3) caring for Fellowship correspondence; (4) notifying persons appointed to committees; (5) maintaining accurate lists of members, visitors, and prospective members; (6) compiling reports; (7) ordering materials; (8) keeping accurate records of attendance at the Sunday morning and evening sessions of the Fellowship, and at other meetings, as necessary; also, if desired, the general supervision of publicity.

The *treasurer* should have integrity. He should be honest, faithful, accurate, and well informed on the budget and financial policies of the Fellowship. He should: (1) keep a neat and clear record of all money received and spent; (2) manage the handling of funds in harmony with the financial policies of the church and of the Fellowship; (3) make itemized financial reports; (4) serve on the budget committee; and (5) encourage the Youth Fellowship members in systematic and sacrificial giving to the church and its world mission.

Commission or committee chairmen

If there are standing commissions or committees with duly elected or appointed chairmen, these chairmen are usually listed as officers of the Fellowship and, as such, share in responsibility with other members of the cabinet for shaping the total program of the Fellowship.

Leaders of special groups within the Fellowship

If *weekday clubs* — such as the Girls' Guild, the Boys' Club, the Scouts, the Y Clubs, the Camp Fire Girls — are to be actively related to other phases of the Youth Fellowship organization and program, they must have youth and adult leaders who are recognized in some way as officers of the Youth Fellowship. It is comparatively easy to do this when there is a church-sponsored Youth Fellowship coeducational club, a Fellowship Guild for Girls, or a Fellowship Boys' Club. In this case the youth leader and the adult counselor are usually accepted as members of the Youth Fellowship cabinet, and share in the programing and planning. When other clubs, representing nondenominational agencies such as the Boy Scouts of America or the YMCA, use the church for their meeting place, it is quite possible to arrange for church sponsorship and to provide for partial or full participation of the youth and adult leaders in the Youth Fellowship cabinet meetings.

If *athletic teams* are organized as part of the Youth Fellowship recreation program, there may be value in having them represented in the cabinet during the period they are functioning. Usually such organization is very simple.

The *youth choir,* instead of establishing an independent organization, should be regarded as a function of the Youth Fellowship, with participation of the director or of a youth representative in the meetings of the cabinet when needed.

The *Sunday church school classes,* if there are several in an age-group department, are usually regarded as study units of the Youth Fellowship and therefore do not ordinarily require the election of a set of officers. However, at times, situations may call for the appointment of a youth representative of each class to serve on the cabinet for shorter or longer periods.

94

THE ADULT COUNSELORS

The Youth Fellowship advisers

Various terms are used for the adult leaders of youth — adviser, counselor, sponsor, superintendent, teacher. The various functions suggested by these terms are all involved to greater or lesser degree in the duties of each of those who work with the Youth Fellowship. The teacher, for example, is at times a leader and adviser in planning, and at times a counselor in guiding individuals. The adviser who works directly with the youth officers in the administrative task needs at various times to display the qualities of a teacher; at other times, those of a counselor; at still others, those of a superintendent.

It is usually desirable for the church to appoint through its board of Christian education, in consultation with the young people, some one person (or a married couple) to serve as the age-group Fellowship adviser (or counselor or sponsor or superintendent). This person, ideally, is assigned responsibility for general oversight of the Youth Fellowship in all its activities. He may serve as: (1) superintendent of the morning department session; (2) sponsor of the evening meeting; (3) adviser to the weekday club groups; and (4) chief counselor to the cabinet. If desired, he may have assistants assigned to any of these functions. This is another point at which the flexibility of the Fellowship idea is an asset. The size of the church and other local circumstances may influence the decision as to the number of advisers and their duties. For example, in small churches the Youth Fellowship adviser may also serve as the teacher of the young people's class; in large churches he may require one or more general assistants and, in addition, have the help of the teachers as counselors to the program area commissions.

Various plans have been developed to maintain the highly important principle of unity in planning through one adult with general oversight, while dividing the responsibilities so as to avoid overburdening any one person. The problem applies to each of the age-group departments or Fellowships (junior high, senior high, and older youth). One approach is represented in this statement:

> "Ideally, for each of the three departments there should be a superintendent and a youth adviser of the church. The superintendent will think of his work as supervision not only in the Sunday church school but also in all other sessions which are felt to be desirable for this age group. This does not mean, however, that the department superintendent must attend all the sessions for the youth of his age group. . . . The youth adviser will work directly with the young people in their various sessions, whether it be Sunday morning, Sunday evening, or in connection with weekday activities. . . . But while the department superintendent has primary responsibility for correlating the efforts of the *adults* who work with the youth of this age group, the adviser has primary responsibility for working with the youth themselves. It is the adviser who will meet with the youth cabinet. He will be present at their social functions and will participate in the weekday projects which grow out of the Sunday evening meetings." [2]

Teachers

The teachers of Sunday morning Fellowship classes in the church school have a primary responsibility for the leadership of the thinking of those in their classes through the use of the study program and the curriculum as approved by the church. This they will do through the use of various methods designed to enlist the interest and participation of the young people. As teachers, they must be prepared to serve also as friendly counselors and guides, and to assist as advisers in general program planning and with specific groups when special assignments are made. For example, the *Handbook*

[2] From *Our Church Plans for Youth*, by Forrest B. Fordham. Copyright, 1953, The Judson Press. Used by permission.

of the Methodist Youth Fellowship states, "Teachers of high school classes may serve also as advisers of program areas. If there is more than one teacher of high school classes, all of them need not attend every council meeting." [3] The publication, *Handbook: Senior High Fellowship,* produced by the Presbyterian Church, U. S., states concerning teachers, "Often in large youth groups they [teachers] may also serve as advisers to the commissions, planning closely with the adult adviser. . . . They will find it helpful to accept invitations to visit Fellowship meetings other than the Sunday morning period whenever possible." [4] Too many other adults should not be present on these occasions.

Leaders of special groups within the Fellowship

Club or Scout leaders. If there are weekday club groups, coeducational or segregated as to sexes — whether a Fellowship Girls' Guild or Boys' Club, a Boy Scout or Girl Scout troop, a YMCA or YWCA or Camp Fire Girls' unit, or some other group using the church as a meeting place — such clubs should be sponsored by the church and should be related to the age-group Fellowship through their leaders. These leaders have the important responsibility of working closely with the Fellowship adviser, the youth cabinet, and the youth work committee of the church, to co-ordinate the youth program, to enrich the club program with moral and spiritual values, and, so far as is possible within the limits of the policies permitted by the national agency of which their club may be a part, to include positive religious emphases in the club activities. Ideally, these leaders should be members of the church, appointed in consultation with the church board of Christian

[3] From *Handbook of the Methodist Youth Fellowship.* Copyright, 1953. Board of Education of the Methodist Church. Used by permission.

[4] From *Handbook: Senior High Fellowship.* Produced by the Presbyterian Church, U. S. Copyright, 1952. John Knox Press. Used by permission.

education. They should be well informed concerning the Fellowship organization and program.

Choir, drama, or other interest groups. Special interest groups of church young people, of whatever nature, should not be established as independent organizations but as activities or functions of the Fellowship. The leaders of these groups should concentrate upon the special interest — music, athletics, drama, craft, or hobby — and upon the activities closely associated with this interest, and should not seek to develop an independent, well-rounded, self-sufficient program of social and other activities. The leaders should be selected in consultation with the young people, and should work closely with the youth cabinet and the adult staff.

The minister or director of Christian education

A highly important leader in the youth program is the minister. He should be a companion, friend, counselor, and guide to the young people themselves and to their adult leaders. He should have a full understanding of the Youth Fellowship movement, its organization and program, and should be an ex-officio member of the cabinet and the leaders' council.

An increasing number of churches employ a trained minister of education, a director of Christian education, or director of youth work. Any such individual should have a large place of leadership in the youth program.

Among the ways in which the minister or director may assist young people are the following: (1) the discovery and enlistment of adult leaders for the youth program; (2) the coaching and training of adult and youth leaders; (3) behind-the-scenes planning, and counseling of leaders; (4) the discovery of weak spots, and suggesting improvement; (5) serving as a resource leader to assist in planning sessions; (6) suggesting literature and other sources for help; (7) assistance in co-ordination of the youth work with the total task of the church; (8) interpreting the youth program to the church, and securing financial and moral support; (9) counseling individuals concerning their spiritual life, their personal problems, their personality growth, leadership, skills, life choices, and vocational outlook; (10) attendance, when possible, at cabinet meetings, retreats, and other planning sessions; (11) attendance, when possible, at Sunday and weekday meetings and social events; (12) supplying spiritual insight and personal leadership, on occasion, in study and discussion meetings, worship services, installations, and retreats.

COMMISSIONS OR COMMITTEES

CHRISTIAN FAITH, CHRISTIAN WITNESS, CHRISTIAN OUTREACH, CHRISTIAN CITIZENSHIP, CHRISTIAN FELLOWSHIP

In considering the structure of the Youth Fellowship, an important question arises: How may the organization provide for thorough study and effective action in the various fields included in the Christian life? One of the best answers is to group these fields into program areas and assign them to commissions or committees. We have already reviewed briefly the significant process by which the separate experiments of the various denominational Youth Fellowships with different but similar commission names were consolidated into the present plan of the five program areas used in common by many of the denominations: *Faith, Witness, Outreach, Citizenship,* and *Fellowship.* In Chapter II on "Whither Bound?" we considered the scope and content of each of these areas. They are important to the program of study and discussion, to the choice of worship themes and materials, and to the development of activity and service projects. In Chapter VI on "The Fellowship at Worship," Chapter VII on "The Fellowship at Study," and Chapter VIII on "The Fellowship in Action," help will be found on ways to use the areas in the Fellowship program.

At this point we are concerned simply with the organizational significance of these areas. There are several possibilities:

(1) the appointment of five commissions or committees, one for each area, each with responsibility
   (a) for developing and carrying through action projects
   (b) for planning and conducting meeting programs and worship services

(2) the appointment of five commissions or committees, each with responsibility for committee work or action projects, but not with direct responsibility for meeting programs and worship services, the latter being handled by a special program committee

(3) the use of the program areas as a basis for broad planning through the cabinet without naming separate committees

In some small groups the third plan is used; in others, commissions made up of one or two persons only are named, or there is a combination of commissions; for example, Faith and Witness, Outreach and Citizenship. Still another plan is to assign one or more commissions to each of the officers. In an average-size group of from twelve to thirty-five members, it is quite feasible to have separate officers and five separate commissions. A plan very widely used is to place each active member on one of the five commissions. Subcommittees may be created if desired, or special committees as needed.

For most Junior High (or Intermediate) Fellowships the program areas, while having value to leaders in broad planning, do not require standing commissions or committees. Instead, special committees are created to carry through projects or discussion units, and are discharged when the project is completed.

100

In churches or denominations not using the five program areas as listed above, these areas have meaning for reference regardless of what plan is followed as to organization.

AGE-GROUP FELLOWSHIPS

Junior High (or Intermediate) Fellowship

This organizational unit is usually made up of those who are in the seventh, eighth, and ninth grades in school, ages approximately 12, 13, and 14. Sometimes, if there is a two-grade public junior high school in the community or there is a four-year high school and no junior high, a two-year Junior High (or Intermediate) Fellowship is established, though it is usually felt to be more satisfactory under such circumstance to maintain a three-year span in the church group.

Junior highs are eager and energetic. They need a church-centered organization which will become their primary loyalty and which will help them to experience life to the full on their own age level. They need to have the fun of choosing their own officers, making their own plans, building and conducting their own programs, taking on and discharging responsibilities, learning from their failures and successes. The Junior High (or Intermediate) Fellowship furnishes such opportunities. It includes all the meetings and activities for this group in the church. If there is only Sunday school, that is the Fellowship, with the teacher or department superintendent as adviser. If four or five or more can be brought together in an evening meeting, this may approximately double for them the amount of time spent in Christian education. For this age group especially, the weekday club groups (whether coeducational or segregated — Girls' Guild, Boys' Club, Scout Troop, Y Club, Camp Fire Girls) are considered important in some churches. If such groups exist, it is de-

101

sirable that they be closely related to other aspects of the Junior High Fellowship program. This applies also to the vacation and weekday church school, the day camp (sleep at home) and the away-from-home camp.

As an organization, the Junior High Fellowship — with all its meetings and activities — functions under the guidance of its youth officers and adult leaders through its cabinet (or council). It works in full co-operation with the other age-group Fellowships in the youth division council, and is under the general guidance of the church board of Christian education.

Senior High (or Senior) Fellowship

This age-group Fellowship is usually made up of those who are in the tenth, eleventh, and twelfth grades in school, ages approximately 15, 16, and 17. Sometimes, if there is no Junior High Fellowship, and especially if there is a four-year senior high school in the community, the ninth-graders are also included.

The Senior High Fellowship provides for a comprehensive program of worship, study, recreation, and service. It offers many opportunities for training in the activities and skills related to the varied meetings and projects of an adequate church program for youth. Even when the number is small there is distinct advantage in having a separate organization to provide more opportunity for training and more specialized study and discussion. There is place for many intergroup activities and events so that young people of the various age groups may become acquainted and may share social and other experiences.

Organizationally, the Senior High Fellowship functions democratically in all its Sunday and weekday meetings and activities under the supervision of its youth officers and adult leaders, through its cabinet (or council). It co-operates fully with the youth division council and with the church board of Christian education.

Older Youth or Student Fellowship

The ages included in this group (beyond high school) differ in various churches, covering late teens and early twenties, approximately 18 to 23, 24, or 25. Likewise, the composition of the group varies widely — students now in college; ex-students, with one or more years of college, perhaps college graduates; nonstudents (without college experience); unemployed or employed (many may be ex-students, some college graduates). Sometimes younger married couples prefer to remain in this group, though usually they move on to a Young Adult Fellowship if there is such a group. When the group is entirely or preponderantly students, it becomes a Student Fellowship, or uses some other appropriate name. When largely nonstudent, it becomes an Older Youth Fellowship.

Through the Older Youth Fellowship, members may express creative ability in planning meetings, discussing vital issues, and carrying through action projects. They may choose to create their own organizational pattern or to adapt general plans to their own needs. They should rely largely upon the leadership of their officers and cabinet, but should have an adult adviser to help maintain stability and continuity of policy. They should work in full co-operation with the youth division council and with the church board of Christian education, and give constructive help to younger groups and in the life of the church generally.

Combined age-group Fellowships

Age groups should not be combined unless really necessary. The physical, intellectual, and social differences between junior and senior highs and between senior highs and older youth are so great that it is usually much more satisfactory to have small groups than to merge merely to get numbers. If groups are combined, there are several possibilities: (1) Junior High — Senior High (sometimes called High School Fellowship); (2) Senior High — Older Youth (sometimes called Older Youth Fellowship, and sometimes Senior Fellowship, depending upon where predominant age and interest lie); (3) Junior High — Senior High — Older Youth (usually called simply Youth Fellowship). In combined groups it is necessary to adapt materials and plans, to provide for varying interests and needs, and to assign leadership responsibility and provide training for all the ages represented.

ORGANIZATIONAL LINKS AND RELATIONSHIPS

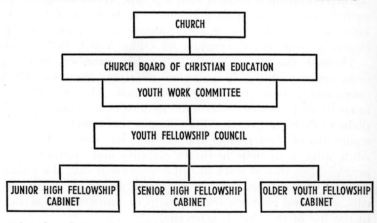

The church board of Christian education

The responsibility of the church itself for formulating broad policies and for giving general guidance and direction to the youth program is expressed usually through some type of church board, or commission, on Christian education. This group functions for the church in determining curriculum and in enlisting and training leaders for all groups. In consultation with the young people, it selects and appoints advisers and teachers; provides budget, materials and equipment; and reviews aims, policies, and plans.

The youth committee of the church

This is usually a subcommittee of the board of Christian education, with a chairman selected from that board or serving ex-officio upon it. The membership of the subcommittee, in a small church, may include all adults who work with youth; in a large church it may include those who serve in an administrative capacity as advisers or superintendents or counselors for junior highs, senior highs, and older youth, or leaders in the club program. The youth chairman of the youth council may serve on the committee; also, in ex-officio capacities, the minister, director of Christian education, and church school superintendent.

The duties of this committee are to serve as liaison between the board of Christian education and the youth council and cabinets, and to act as a focal point for planning by adults of their part in the youth program. Many problems and plans will be reviewed, such as leadership and curriculum needs, grouping and grading, rooms and equipment, resources and supplies, seasonal observances and special days, coaching and training opportunities. Policies and basic decisions will be referred to the youth council, age-group cabinets, and the board of Christian education, for decision.

The Youth Fellowship council

This is the organizational unit of the young people themselves in which the age-group cabinets or councils are represented, and plans are made for the program of the youth division of the church. This council (1) co-ordinates the work of the department cabinets; (2) stimulates youth participation in all church events, all youth activities, worship, and other joint sessions; (3) plans all youth activities, worship, and other joint sessions, projects, events, and emphases for the junior high, senior high and older youth age groups; and (4) works in close co-operation with the youth committee and the board of Christian education.

Membership in this council may be made up of three youth representatives from each of the age-group Fellowships, plus the department advisers or counselors (one from each Fellowship); the chairman of the youth committee or the superintendent of the youth division of the church, and an adult representative of the club work. Usually the adults do not vote but are available for counsel.

The age-group cabinets (junior high, senior high, older youth)

The general elective officers of each age-group Fellowship (president, vice-president, secretary, treasurer), plus the commission or committee chairmen and the adult advisers, generally make up a cabinet, an executive committee, or a council. This group is responsible for co-ordinating all Fellowship activities (Sunday morning, evening, and weekdays), and for general planning and promotion of the program. If there are separate age-group Fellowships (Junior High, Senior High, Older Youth) there is usually a cabinet or council for each Fellowship. These cabinets are extremely important links in the Youth Fellowship organizational structure. It is essential that they meet regularly, usually once a month; that the president and adviser prepare a docket of items to be discussed; that careful assignments be made; that records be kept of decisions; and that each officer share fully in the plans.

Interchurch co-operation

Denominational. The Youth Fellowship movement has strong denominational ties. Usually there are regional, state, and national units of the denominational Youth Fellowship organization, with youth officers and significant interchurch camps, conferences, banquets, institutes, caravans, work camps, coaching clinics, and co-operative projects. These furnish opportunities for young people to receive inspiration and training, and to feel the sense of fellowship in the wider scope of the Christian enterprise.

Interdenominational. As we have seen, the Youth Fellowship movement provides a channel for co-operation among denominational youth organizations which share similar aims, terminology, and philosophy. For example, the young people of the churches of many communities co-operate in Youth Week observance, in fellowship occasions, and in joint projects. The national expression of this co-operation is the United Christian Youth Movement with which are affiliated some forty or more denominations in the United States and Canada, and such agencies as the YMCA, YWCA, Christian Endeavor, Boy Scouts of America, Girl Scouts of America, Camp Fire Girls. The local expression of this co-operation is the community Christian Youth Council, with representation of each local church Youth Fellowship. It affords excellent possibilities for exchanging ideas, sharing experiences of inspiration and training, and co-operating in common projects of community service.

Chapter VI

THE FELLOWSHIP AT WORSHIP

"God is spirit, and those who worship him must worship in spirit and truth." [1]

COME, LET US WORSHIP

Central in every individual's life

There is no escaping the glorious fact that the Divine Being who has created and maintained this infinitely vast and complicated universe has, in his divine providence, created man with the capacity to worship. Man has the ability to pray, to express joy and adoration, to seek forgiveness, to receive spiritual renewal and power to live aright — in short, to share fellowship with God himself.

Those times when we feel ourselves to be at our very best — when we enjoy a beautiful symphony or a sunset, when we feel spiritually bound to others of like-minded ideals and purposes, when we pour out our hearts in penitence and feel the burden of guilt lifted from us, when we make a great choice leading to some unselfish course of service — these are times when we are in the mood of worship. Because the need for worship is central in every individual's life, God has given us a company of believers in him who share fellowship in worship. God has also instructed us to set aside a day in each week largely for this purpose.

Basic to the youth program

Worship is of primary importance to the youth program. Some youth may not have discovered this. They may have been going through the motions without a real appreciation

[1] John 4:24.

108

and the value of worship. Or they may have ̷hasizing talk about religion, sociability, fun, ᴐn, or even religious activity and meetings, without ̷onted with God in worship. To do justice to the ϩ of youth, the Youth Fellowship program must be ̷evoted to worship.

̷ted to the total church program

Church family worship is primary. Young people need the experience of worshiping God with all members of the church family, preferably in the family pew, or in groups seated among the adult worshipers. This experience they need for various reasons: (1) to help in establishing a lifelong habit of fellowship with God in worship; (2) to sense their full identification with the total body of the church; (3) to feel a strong sense of loyalty to the minister and to the church; (4) to gain an appreciation for the maturity and strength of corporate worship. The church sanctuary is usually the most suitable place to meet God and to discover that true worship always is related to him. For these reasons the regular church services of worship should be a primary factor in the experience of all young people.

Youth needs training in worship. Training for and in worship is an important part of the church's program of Christian education. Involved in this training is general instruction in the aims and characteristics of worship and concerning the elements of worship which help to make us aware of God. Much more than this general training is needed — especially for junior highs. Specific training is necessary in understanding the great hymns of the church, the meaning of the words, the use of the music; the language of prayer and the various forms of prayer; and the different parts of the worship service and their purpose.

The Youth Fellowship

A large place in the Youth Fellowship program each year, or within a three-year cycle, should be given to the study of worship and the training for worship. This might well include the learning each year of ten or a dozen new hymns chosen because of the quality of the music, the abiding worth of the words. A good project which many Youth Fellowships have carried through successfully is the "Hymn of the Month" plan — using throughout each month an outstanding hymn, frequently one not too well known, with interpretation of its history and meaning, so as to make it a permanent part of the experience of each member of the group. Several books on hymn stories and appreciation are available, and a number of fine books on worship, such as *Restoring Worship* by Clarice Bowman.

The training in worship which young people receive should not be limited to preparation for participation in the church worship services. Training should help them to share in their own graded and sharply focused age-group worship experiences. Junior highs, seniors, and older youth all need to learn how to read Scripture, to pray in public, to plan and conduct worship services, to approach God with reverent and receptive hearts. It is likewise important to consider each separate member of the group and to find ways of helping him to achieve knowledge and appreciation of worship, judgment in choice and organization of material, poise in leadership, and sincerity in spirit. Thus preparation is made for effective lifelong churchmanship, which is a concern of all youth leaders.

Specialized worship is helpful for youth. Much worship is universal in its appeal and therefore fits both young people and adults. But many of the deeper needs of young people of the different age levels are highly individual and special to youth. Young people need to be approached through wor-

110

ship experiences which are tailor-made to fit them closely, or, if custom-made, at least in specific sizes. A twelve-year-old would look very awkward in the suit of a twenty-three-year-old, and would feel and act just as awkward in a worship service which did not fit his spiritual needs.

Junior highs need experiences of worship which make God real to them and cause them to reach toward him. For them, life is present tense, not future. The profound realities of the Christian faith should be expressed in terms understandable to junior highs and applicable to their daily lives.

Senior highs also need help through worship in being confronted with God, in learning to hear and heed his voice. It is important that their worship be real to them, not just a mood, a setting, or a program. It is likewise desirable that worship bear fruit in changed lives, not merely in retreat into the sanctuary or to the mountaintop.

The Student Fellowship program should provide mature worship experiences which will expose graduate and undergraduate students to the great heritage of prayer and devotional thought, and to social and biographical material. Relevant to the lives of rural youth are hymns, Scripture, and illustrations revealing God in nature and showing man's place as worker with him. Industrial youth need similar inspiration for facing, with God, daily life in factory, shop, or office.

TYPES OF WORSHIP FOR YOUTH

Personal devotions

Though the presence of others and the use of the facilities and leadership resources of the church usually help in worship, it still is possible for an individual to meet God in the quiet of his own room, in surroundings of beauty in nature, or even in the midst of need on a city street . . . in a factory

. . . on the farm . . . in a school. The cultivation of habits of daily prayer and meditation, Bible reading and study, and the use of devotional literature are of utmost importance for Youth Fellowship emphasis. Young people, active in denominational and interdenominational leadership, have themselves stressed this in their national and area plans, and they have offered practical suggestions to encourage the development of devotional disciplines.

Informal group devotions

Informal worship is often effective and meaningful, for it may arise from a fresh and vital experience and come as a spontaneous and sincere expression of devotion and dedication. Such occasions may follow a happy social event, a picnic, a hike, a fun program; or an absorbing discussion, a retreat, or planning session; or time of fellowship at the church, in a home, or around a campfire. It may take the form of the family altar, morning watch, a prayer hour, evening vespers, or perhaps quite frequently a devotional period or fellowship circle prior to or following the Sunday evening meeting or the weekday club. This type of worship may take on an order of procedure, or can be quite spontaneous. If a prearranged plan of procedure is desired, there might be time provided for: (1) silent recollection of God's presence; (2) a responsive reading; (3) the singing or reading of one or more hymns; (4) an extempore spoken prayer, or sentence expressions of dedication, consecration or petition.

Planned youth services of worship

These usually have a specific *theme* around which all the elements of worship are centered. The Scripture, music, poetry, prayer, meditations, audio-visuals, or stories are on the central theme or subject. It is needful that the themes deal with areas of experience appropriate for worship, and of interest and value to junior highs, senior highs, or older youth. The material used in worship should apply to them and to their real needs.

Planned worship services are usually conducted in a carefully arranged setting, often with a worship center. The atmosphere, the surroundings, and the setting are all incidental to the purpose of true worship, yet the assurance of successful worship is usually that there is planned expression, and opportunity for individual and collective participation. These occasions for participation include the singing of hymns, silent and spoken prayer, litanies, responsive readings, choric reading, the offering.

In theme and content, planned youth services of worship may be *related to the study-discussion units,* the objectives of Christian education, and the five program areas of the Youth Fellowship. The services should grow out of needs and experiences in these areas. Many of the aims of Christian education, especially those which deal with the feelings, the attitudes, and the choices of life, are achieved better through meaningful worship experience than in any other way.

Youth's place in the church worship

The youth of a church are a vital part of the fellowship of any congregation. It is most urgent to have junior highs develop a sense of oneness with the church fellowship early in their experience, and for this feeling to be intensified as they grow older. A wise minister keeps in mind the youth of the church as he plans public worship. It is not essential that youth be set apart or singled out for special attention. If the church services of worship are truly meaningful and universal in their appeal because of beauty, dignity, sincerity, unity, and drama (in the finer sense), they should have special

H 113

appeal to youth. Youth should feel that they belong to the family of God, that they share in corporate expressions of the Christian fellowship, that the worship voices their own feelings and responses to God, and that God speaks to their own hearts and lives in worship.

Now and then, in some churches, it may be in order to give opportunity for youth participation in special ways: sharing as ushers; singing in the choir; representing youth on the church boards; serving as hosts, hostesses, or greeters. Special assignments for participation on special occasions — such as Christian Education Week, Christmas, Race Relations Sunday, Youth Week, Family Week, Commencement Sunday — may be undertaken by youth. In small churches, youth participation is especially appropriate, particularly in Sunday evening worship services, which tend to be more informal. This may include youth choirs, choric speech, drama, worship, and individual leadership in Scripture, prayer, and responses.

During the annual observance of Youth Week several years ago, the author attended a large church in Washington, D. C. — having congressmen, judges, and other prominent persons in the congregation. The entire service was conducted by youth. The choir was directed, the organ was played, the service was conducted, the offering collected, the sermon preached — all most effectively by young people. Incidentally, over three hundred young people participated during Youth Week. Nearly every activity of the church was undertaken by young people — janitor service, counting the money, hospital visitation (certain cases only), and the teaching of all church school classes — after months of preparation. Many have found their way into church vocations and have discovered qualifications for lay leadership as a result of such practical training.

CHECK SHEET FOR EVALUATING WORSHIP

1. Is it directed Godward?
2. Does it involve surrender to God and response to him?
3. Is it genuine and real, vitally related to the needs of youth?
4. Does it make effective use of the various elements of worship?
5. Does it have unity—a clear aim and central theme?
6. Does it reach a spiritual high point?
7. Does it make fresh appeal while expressing familiar experiences?
8. Are the physical surroundings such as to create reverence and reality?
9. Are appropriate aids used to produce a worshipful mood and a vital experience?

ELEMENTS OF WORSHIP

The call to worship

The call — "come worship" — is a summons away from the noisy, hectic confusion of a secular world into the union of thought and spirit of the group, a bringing of minds and hearts into focus upon God. Its purpose is to set a tone or mood, and to open a gateway into the life of the spirit. Scripture verses, particularly those from the Book of Psalms, help in accomplishing this purpose. Sometimes a hymn, a poetic phrase or verse, or a meaningful quotation may be used. Using the familiar has value, but there is merit at times in acquainting young people with new passages of Scripture and fresh poetry. Here are two examples of calls to worship: "Be still, and know that I am God. . . . I am exalted in the earth!" (Ps. 46:10); "O come, let us worship and bow down, let us kneel before the Lord, our Maker!" (Ps. 95:6). In an evening Fellowship meeting, the leader may quote from a hymn such as "Day is Dying in the West." Then the entire group may respond, singing words of the chorus, "Holy, holy, holy, Lord God of hosts." Psalm 24:1-5 is appropriate as a call to worship when read antiphonally or by a verse-speaking choir.

Hymns

Of inestimable value, in the worship experiences of youth are hymns. Through the wedding of good music to fine poetry, and group expression of high thoughts, noble aspirations, and deep feelings, the entire personality of each individual may be lifted toward God, and the entire group may achieve a solidarity of fellowship and dedication. Good hymns have important functions. They promote understanding of Christian truth; increase conviction in the Christian faith; develop appreciation of Christian ideals and attitudes; provide opportunity for Christian fellowship; encourage awareness of God and receptivity to his will; become a means for confession of guilt and failure, of expression of joy and thankfulness; stimulate right Christian choices, and sound and sustained Christian action.

In the planning of worship services, much skill is required in the selection of the best hymns for youth, for the specific theme, and for the particular place and purpose of the service. If it be true that second only to the Bible in the Christian education of youth is the hymnbook, then it is of utmost importance that the best possible choice of a regular youth hymnbook be made and of the hymns which are to find their way into the life experience of growing adolescents.

Among the tests of good hymns for youth are these: 1. Does the poetry express meaningful ideas in language which is beautiful, dignified, and effective? 2. Is the imagery appropriate for worship, and true to the Christian heritage? 3. Is the theology in accord with basic Christian teachings? 4. Are the ideas expressed relevant to the problems and needs of youth — junior highs, seniors, older youth? 5. Are they expressed in language which has meaning for them? 6. Is the music appropriate for the worship of God — does it have beauty, dignity, and strength? 7. Is it singable? 8. Does it possess enduring worth? 9. Do the music and the words say the same thing — that is, in its spirit and feeling, is the music religious?

Special music

Vocal and instrumental music add greatly to the beauty and effectiveness of worship experiences, and afford a way to enlist the talents of young people who have acquired these special skills. Participants should be encouraged to prepare well, and to make their parts not performances but acts of worship. Through atmosphere music during the service (the prelude, postlude, offering, silent prayer, and so forth), the rich heritage of great religious music may become a factor in the experience of all who worship.

Prayer

At the heart of all worship experience, essential to individual growth and fellowship that is truly Christian, is prayer. This highest of all relationships — between finite human beings and infinite God — should not be approached carelessly or insincerely. Various forms of prayer may provide for meaningful participation: silent prayer, directed prayer (with suggested thoughts from the leader), musical accompaniment to the reading of a prayer poem, sentence prayers, reading of a written prayer, extempore prayer, prayer hymn, litany of dedication or of praise.

Scripture

Worship provides an opportunity to relive and re-experience the joy, gratitude, penitence, hope, and consecration of those who have sought and found God, have heard his voice, and have seen with clear insight deeply into the nature of man and the problems of existence, as revealed supremely in the

117

Scriptures. Through worship, the living message of the Bible becomes a vital force in the present-day experience of youth. Many of the most appealing passages — from the Book of Psalms, for example — may best be brought to youth through worship, and may be used in a variety of ways in services. The Bible is often taken for granted through familiarity. It should be read clearly, with smoothness, intelligence, and color. Using it in different ways, from time to time, will make it more effective. Among such ways are: a musical setting, a dialogue, a dramatic background or setting, a verse-speaking choir, or the use of costume. Usually a Scripture passage holds the key to the central thought of the chosen theme. In addition, there may often be other ways of using the Bible, such as litanies, responsive readings, calls to worship and to service, scriptural sentences of affirmation.

The spoken word or special presentation

The talk or meditation, the story or dramatic episode, the audio-visual, or other presentation should be related to the theme and appropriate to the age-group level and experience. This presentation needs to be well prepared, sincere, and a genuine act of worship. The meditation is very effective, even though brief, in making explicit the implications of the theme. It has value because it directs thought, increases understanding, and stimulates feeling. Stories, dramas, picture interpretations, or audio-visuals, have the advantage of making personal involvement easier through appeal to the emotions. These procedures, going beyond the realm of the purely factual or logical into the realm of the feelings, change attitudes and conduct.

Young people may creatively develop various means of drama-worship — simple costumes, brief episodes, dialogues, dramatic incidents with appropriate background and properties. They may adopt some of the newer techniques of drama-worship — verse-speaking choir, rhythm choir, "readers," "voices," "spokesmen," "questioners," or "interpreters," without the necessity of costumes and exact memorization of lines. Sometimes participants are placed in the audience or at unusual positions in the room. Inspirational colored slide sets or motion pictures are used effectively, sometimes with the help of wire or tape recorder, or record player.

An effective drama-worship service was produced by young people in the author's church on the theme "Right or Wrong?" Many of the participants appeared in dramatic episodes. Others, placed at different points in the audience, at one point broke in, each in turn, with the words, "Is it I?"

The response through group participation

The call to worship assumes a real and vital response to the living God, not merely disinterested observation or passive listening. Without the surrender of mind and heart to God, there can be no worship. The response may come in a number of ways — through unspoken prayer and commitment, through singing, through unison prayer, responsive reading of Scripture and litanies. There may be provided sentences of dedication, and also acts of commitment — especially an offering.

PRINCIPLES OF EFFECTIVENESS IN WORSHIP

The necessity for relevance—meaning, reality

Worship, if it is to be more than form, must be relevant to the lives and the problems of those who live in our contemporary world. Part of its value lies in its ability to lift them above their surroundings and, in the presence of God, gain perspective, poise, and power.

The place of unity—value of an aim, a theme

The great advantage of having a clear aim and a well-stated theme is that they contribute to the achievement of a single, unified effect. Each worship service should seek to accomplish something definite — a new awareness of some aspect or purpose of God, a change of attitude toward people or things, a prompting to serve or to share.

The need for order—progression, balance, climax

Every good worship service has a plan — not merely a series of worship elements stuck together, but the various parts arranged in a logical order. A study of good worship experience reveals a progression; for example, from reverent adoration and praise to confession, and thence to petition and dedication. In most worship services it is essential to maintain a balance between the various elements, and quite desirable for the progression to reach a high point or climax. Often this climax involves some act of surrender, or affirmation, or response, in which all may share — audibly or silently.

The value of the familiar, the novel

In effective worship a good balance is maintained between the new and the old, the novel or unusual and the familiar. Great care is exercised to avoid, on the one hand, the repetition of familiar forms until they become dull and ineffective, and on the other hand, the use of the unfamiliar in such form that it distracts from the mood of worship, or the novel in such a way as to attract undue attention to itself. Often there is great merit in using a familiar order of service to increase a sense of reality and to reduce the amount of concentration required upon the forms. Again, there is great value in the forcefulness and the reality which come from that which is fresh, compelling new attention and response.

The importance of suitable physical conditions

God is a God of order and of beauty. His worship should be conducted in an orderly manner and in a setting which suggests his presence. Everything possible should be done to remove distraction, eliminate disturbances and interruptions, decrease bodily discomfort (through air, temperature, light and seating), and to create surroundings of beauty and meaning. Much is being done to provide rooms for worship and Christian teaching which are well arranged as to lighting, heating, seating, and attractive in their color schemes and equipment. Many churches can redecorate old rooms, and solve awkward problems by special draperies, panels, and furnishings. Of great importance is an adequate worship center, preferably one which is subject to change and variety.

AIDS IN WORSHIP

Worship centers

The increasing use of the worship center in the less ritualistic denominations is an indication of the value of the eye appeal in worship. Such a center is not a shrine. It is a place of beauty and order which directs and focuses thought and attention, helping to create the mood of worship. Psychologically, it acts as a unifying and centralizing factor for individuals who come to worship from all kinds of circumstances. The starting point is usually a wall upon which or against which may be set, permanently or temporarily, panels, cloth or other hangings or drapes, or other furnishings. Ideally, with young people the worship center should be such that it may be completely or partially changed from time to time during the church year. It can create specialized atmosphere appropriate to varied themes.

For most services, simplicity is an asset — one large candle or perhaps three with an evergreen spray; an open Bible with a bouquet of flowers; the cross in one of its many forms; a globe with a cross; a beautiful religious painting appropriately mounted or framed. For special themes and occasions, young people with resourcefulness may supply or arrange meaningful and symbolic objects — a stained-glass window; a lighthouse; an altar of stones such as Abraham erected; Easter lilies; a bundle of wheat; fall vegetables and fruits; a Christmas crèche; a new year's bell; a madonna; a beautiful ceramic; a loaf of bread; a picture of hands — at toil in prayer, outstretched, or clasped; a map with streamers to a church spire or a cross; a model church.

Hymnbooks

In recent years the different denominations have produced excellent hymnbooks appropriate for young people. These books contain the great hymns of the church, the rightful heritage of every Christian, plus the hymns which have special meaning for youth. Hymn appreciation, both of the new and of the familiar, should be a regular experience in all youth groups. Each group should collect good hymnbooks, both those for youth and those for general purposes, and make wide use of the poetry, music, responsive readings, litanies, calls to worship, and benedictions which they contain.

Picture file

A picture file and folio should be in each youth department, or at least available to all. The mounting size should be uniform but permit pictures of various sizes. The larger pictures may be placed in the folio for protection. A standard picture frame the size of the mounting can be fitted with a removable back so that pictures can be readily changed.

Current and back issues of national magazines should be canned for reproductions of suitable pictures, and catalogues secured from publishers and distributors. Guy Rowe's contemporary set, *Portraits of Old Testament Characters,* and Albert E. Bailey's set, *Christ in Recent Art,* are highly stimulating to youth. At least one good picture, in large size, framed, should be on a wall of each department and classroom. Good examples are Zimmerman's *Christ and the Fishermen;* Burnand's *Go Preach;* Taylor's *Christ in Gethsemane;* Sallman's *Head of Christ;* Hofmann's *The Rich Young Ruler* and *Christ in Gethsemane.*

Poetry, quotation, and story file

Poetry, stories, and pointed quotations are so effective in worship experience that they should be used frequently. A great convenience is a file, on standard-size cards, containing a wide assortment of devotional and inspirational materials. Beautiful, meaningful poetry, stories, illustrations, and quotations may be found in the daily newspapers, magazines, religious periodicals, and books. Get the clipping habit; save everything worth saving, classify it, and *use it.*

The worship bookshelf

Like tools to the carpenter are books and other resource materials to the leader of youth. For inexperienced young people and adult leaders, several fine books exist which contain services carefully worked out. As skill is developed, these and other books containing religious poetry, stories, prayers, and biographical incidents may be used as resource material. To these may be added several good hymnbooks, collections of daily devotions, inspirational books on the Bible and on the Christian life, books on how to prepare worship services, and a file of magazines containing worship programs.

Chapter VII

THE FELLOWSHIP AT STUDY

"Take my yoke upon you, and learn from me . . ." [1]

THE QUEST FOR KNOWLEDGE

Abraham Lincoln is reported to have said, "I will study and get ready, and maybe my chance will come." Every young person has, or should have, this opportunity — to get ready for life. There is so much to learn — about God, the Bible, the life and teachings of Jesus, the history and program of the church, the Christian faith and its application to everyday living. We all must start early, and keep on working at the task as long as we live. To be religious is much more than to acquire facts, but it certainly includes knowledge.

How can we organize the study program of the Youth Fellowship so that the dozen or so years involved for each individual will provide for a progressive, comprehensive series of studies which will meet his needs?

THE CHURCH IS A SCHOOL

The Great Commission of Christ emphasizes the fact that the church is a school of Christian living, a fellowship of learners who are instructed, "Go therefore and make disciples . . . teaching them to observe all that I have commanded you . . ." This commission still applies.

STUDY IS RELATED TO THE WHOLE PROGRAM

The Youth Fellowship class in the morning church school

Study is traditionally the primary function of the Sunday

[1] Matthew 11:29.

morning Youth Fellowship class in the church school. For this reason, the adult leader of the class is referred to as teacher. The time is largely devoted to lessons. Much thought is assigned by the national denominational editorial departments to the development of vitally interesting lesson materials. The local church board of Christian education and the youth counselors see to it that these materials are used with intelligent imagination. When this is done, study becomes an exciting weekly event.

Study in the Sunday evening meeting

The Youth Fellowship evening meeting is also an occasion for study. Usually this study differs in a number of important ways from that of the morning session of the Fellowship:

1. There is relatively more youth participation, and less direct adult leadership.

2. There is more emphasis upon varied program features.

3. The study emphasis is sometimes incidental instead of primary.

4. The "lesson material" is often more topical, dealing with problems supplemental to those treated in the morning. The study-discussion units are often of shorter duration.

5. Each entire age-group Fellowship usually meets as a whole instead of in small class groups.

6. There is sometimes a closer tie-up of the study-discussion to action projects than in the morning session.

Special study groups and experiences

Study is by no means limited to the regular Sunday sessions. Many Youth Fellowships find it feasible to schedule special weekday study groups or to use extra sessions, such as weekday clubs, for study purposes. Sometimes these study groups run continuously on a weekly basis throughout the year;

sometimes on a short-term basis, for three months, for si
weeks, or on an intensive basis during Christmas or Easte
vacation or over a weekend. Some communities sponsor weel
day religious education classes in the churches on release
time from the public schools for the junior high or the junio
and senior high ages, using special religious education cu
ricula prepared for this purpose. In many churches the junio
highs are a regular part of the vacation church school; i
some they share in day-camp experiences. The study progran
of the interchurch camp or youth conference is likewise
part of the local church curriculum. Some churches sponso
teen-age classes before or after school or on Saturday; other
have a Bible study or other class running parallel to th
weekly church prayer meeting, or preceding or following i
Many Student Fellowships find it possible to schedule be
tween-Sunday classes at some hour of the day or evening, o
or off campus. The revival of interest among youth in Bibl
study and in contemporary theological thinking has led t
the establishing of many such groups. The increasing interes
in the cell (yoke) group movement and in the establishing o
small group "redemptive fellowships" has given encourage
ment to study of prayer techniques, spiritual disciplines, bibli
cal teachings, and social problems. Some groups have devotec
themselves to the serious study of religious music, contem
porary literature, or current events.

The interrelatedness of study and action

Most individuals and groups study best when there is
strong *motive for study*. Often the motive is strongest whet
the aim is not merely to *know* but to *act,* to do somethin
about it. The desire to meet a need, to solve a problem, t
carry through a plan, an event or a project which sound
interesting, may lead to a great deal of study without ful

wareness that this is true. Action, to be intelligent and
ffective, must be based on knowledge; knowledge, to be best
bsorbed and retained, must be applied. Hence the program
f study and action must, of necessity, be interrelated. An
nterracial group of youth "Summer Service Projectors" dis-
overed this one summer in Harlem when they started to work
s club leaders and teachers of children in vacation schools.
nherent in the tasks to be performed were the demands for
tudy of methods and materials for teaching, of psychology,
nd of social conditions. This led to consultations with expe-
ienced leaders, the study of textbooks, and observation field
rips.

AREAS OF STUDY

The five program areas

The five areas of emphasis for Youth Fellowships, already
discussed in this book, are valuable as aids in the grouping
nd highlighting of areas for study and action. It is impor-
ant for each leader and each young person to have a working
nowlege of the scope of each in order to use them effectively
n programing. They are especially useful for Sunday eve-
ing and weekday study-discussion units.

1. *Christian Faith.* The wide scope and significance of
his area for Christian education is evident in a list of such
ields of study as these:

Christian Beliefs, The Creeds and Their Meaning for Today, The
Christian Heritage, The Protestant Message, Denominational Convictions
nd Practices, Comparative Religions, Personal Christian Commitment,
What It Means to Become a Christian, Disciplines of the Religious Life,
Personal Enrichment and Growth, Developing Christian Habits, The Life
f Prayer in a World of Science, The Nature and Meaning of Worship,
Ways of Worshiping, Effective Ways of Reading and Studying the Bible,
Christian Moral Standards in Daily Living, Understanding and Practicing
he Christian Life, The Meaning of Church Membership.

2. *Christian Witness*. This area may well include such im portant fields of study as:

Sharing Our Faith with Others, How to Carry on Religious Conversa tions, Leading Others to Christ, Personal and Group Evangelism, Wit nessing Through the Stewardship of Time, Talents and Money, Church manship, My Christian Witness in Youth Fellowship Activities, Oppor tunities for Volunteer Service of Christ in My Church, Witnessing Through My Vocation, The Calling of the Christian, Vocational Oppor tunities and Qualifications, Christian Ideals in Lay Occupations, Oppor tunities in Church Vocations, How to Discover My Lifework, Preparing to Make My Life Count, Biblical Teachings Regarding Work and Vocation, The Christian Philosophy of Work, Biographical Studies of Christian Witnesses.

3. *Christian Outreach*. This area may provide for such fields of study as:

The World Mission of the Christian Church, The History of th Missionary Enterprise, The New Testament Church, The Early Centurie of Christian Expansion, The Protestant Reformation, The Lives of Missionary Pioneers, Contemporary Problems of World Christianity Achievements in Home Missions, The Church in American Life, Th Ecumenical Movement, Christian World-mindedness, Relief and Recon struction Through Interchurch Aid, Christian Foundations for Peace and World Order.

4. *Christian Citizenship*. This area may involve such vita fields of study as:

Understanding My Community, The Christian Good Neighbor Policy Christian Citizenship in My Own Church, Christianizing Race Relations Understanding and Working with Other Faiths, Intercultural Relation ships, Christianizing the Social Order, Christianity in Business Life Christianity in Labor Relations, The Christian Approach to Social Prob lems (juvenile delinquency, alcohol, dope addiction, gambling, employ ment, economic justice, public health, housing, migrant workers, and displaced persons), The Social Teachings of the Bible, Christian Pioneer for Social Justice.

128

5. *Christian Fellowship*. This important area may provide for such fields of study as:

The Meaning of the Christian Fellowship, The Local Church as a Fellowship, The Fellowship Cell Movement, Making More Real Friends, How to Get Along with People, Boy and Girl Relationships (Christian standards in dating), From Friendship to Marriage, Christian Ideals in Love and Marriage, Christianity in Home Life, Christian Standards in Recreation, The Christian Use of Leisure, Creative Arts and Hobbies, Denominational Co-operation, Interdenominational Fellowship.

The major objectives of Christian education

Study areas used most widely in preparing units for the Sunday morning church school curricula are those based upon the major objectives of Christian education, defined in some detail in Chapter II. Though formulations of these objectives differ widely, some elements are common to most statements. These objectives are somewhat less functional in wording than the five program areas. They have the distinct advantage of emphasizing the content of the religious life and experience — in terms of God, Christ, the Bible, the church, personal growth, and relationship to others. They permit the organization of biblical and other study material along clear lines, and offer a wide choice of vital themes for study units. In some materials more than one major objective may be represented.

SPECIAL PROBLEMS AND NEEDS

A few special problems and areas of need justify extra attention in this book, and strong emphasis in the regular curriculum and in supplemental study-discussion units.

Personal religious living

This approach to study is true to the Christian heritage and to the needs of youth in that it combines so-called "per-

sonal religion" with daily living. It has the merit of empha
sizing the understanding of self, the use of spiritual resource
and disciplines, and the practical applications of these t
personal conduct. We have reviewed some of the fascinating
fields for study in our consideration of the program area
"Christian Faith."

Friendship, marriage, and home life

This area is at the top of the list of interests of most young
people, though not often at the top of the church's study
themes. The *Handbook of the Methodist Youth Fellowshi*
says to intermediates: "*First,* you want to be recognized as a
person. Each of you wants to become a person who is wanted
and needed, someone who has a real place in the scheme o
things. *Then,* you want affection and understanding from
your family and friends." [2] To older youth it says, "You need
a group where you might find the right person for a life com
panion. You also need a group to pal around with. . . . You
have been asking questions about love, courtship, marriage
sex." [2] The church is the most logical institution to deal with
personal relations, sex education, and preparation for family
life, yet much of the education which young people receive
on these vital and highly emotional problems comes from
other sources.

Christian vocation

Here is another high spot of need. Some young people may
be less acutely interested than others, partly because they are
drifting. Some are unaware that the church has important
things to say about their lifework even though they are not
considering a "church vocation." The next reformation may
well come through a rediscovery of the New Testament con-

[2] From *Handbook of the Methodist Youth Fellowship.* Copyright, 1953. The Meth
odist Publishing House. Used by permission.

cept of the calling of the Christian — to devote *all* of life to the doing of the will of God — and the application of this revolutionary purpose to the Christianizing of all occupations.

Social education and action

As young people mature, they become aware of others and of the vexing problems in human relationships. The courageous spirit of Jesus, of the Old Testament prophets, and of the Christian pioneers of recent decades is urgently needed in applying Christian principles to the issues of today. Christian youth are challenged to supply venturesome spirit and prophetic insight to the solving of social problems and the producing of intergroup and international co-operation. The church must give them the opportunity to learn the facts, to consider the implications of the Christian gospel of love, and to apply Christian insight through constructive action. This assumes that junior highs will be alerted to the practical issues of their world through clear but stimulating study. Senior highs will discuss realistically the religious significance of these vital issues which so deeply affect human personality. Older youth — students and employed — will be helped to take the lead in intelligent Christian action based upon thorough study.

The church and its world mission

Many fields of study for youth relate to the church and its world task. These include not only the heritage of the past but also an understanding of the unique nature and mission of the church today, the achievements and the limitations of the denominations and the agencies for interchurch co-operation, and the obligations and privileges of churchmanship. They also involve an understanding of the ecumenical movement and its tangible expression in the World Council of

Churches, the National Council of Churches, the state and cit or community councils. The study program should includ training of all young people in missionary knowledge and i world-mindedness, in the skills and insights needed for thei functioning as intelligent lay members of the church.

The Bible

The revival of interest among youth in serious Bible stud is most encouraging. This interest needs to be supportec through regular and special study units dealing with sucl themes as:

The Origin and Nature of the Bible, Old Testament Beginnings, Th Story of the Hebrew People, The Great Religious Ideas in the Ol Testament, The Prophets and Their Messages, The Life of Christ, Th Life and Letters of Paul, The Teachings of Jesus, Human Nature in th Bible, The Bible as Literature, How We Got Our Bible, The Fascinating Story of Bible Translations, The Bible as a Source Book for Christian Living, The Intensive Study of Books of the Bible.

Such units will strengthen the study of various passage used in curriculum units dealing with other objectives o Christian education, and will help to make the Bible a living book in the life of youth today.

Christian beliefs

Among junior highs, seniors, and older youth, a large place must be found for the study of the Christian faith itself. Much of this study will be incorporated in units dealing with various portions of the Bible or with church history. Some of it will be devoted to specific doctrines, or to the fields for study listed under the program area, "Christian Faith." If strong, well-grounded Christians, capable of influencing others, are to be produced by the church's youth program, Christian theology and its terms must be at least as well understood as many of the technical fields of scientific exploration and achievement.

THE AGE-GROUP STUDY PROGRAM

Junior highs

These boys and girls are eager to learn and quick to "catch on" when there is good guidance, but also quick to jump to wrong conclusions when without sufficient data or experience. A skillful and resourceful teacher or counselor is a spiritual lifesaver. He needs a sense of humor and the ability to start minds on a quest in an adventurous spirit.

The regular denominational lesson materials for junior highs include units giving primary emphasis to certain of the areas of study mentioned in this chapter, and secondary emphasis to others. The alert leader uses these materials creatively when he adapts them to fit the needs of his own group. He makes them come alive by putting his own spirit and experience into them. There are lessons to be learned by early adolescents concerning God, Christ, the Bible, the church, the Christian faith, and the Christian way of life which are part of a progressive program of Christian growth. The teacher or leader should help those in the group to see how the lessons relate one to the other. In a given week the Sunday morning and evening studies and those undertaken in the between-Sunday meetings and in extra sessions such as camp and the V.C.S. need not necessarily be closely related. But in the long run they should fit into a correlated plan.

The questionnaire, or interest finder, is a useful device to discover interests. The results are helpful in planning meetings. In the author's church, fifty-two junior highs, asked to check "the ten topics you like best" in a list under consideration, answered in part as follows:

How to Choose and Live with Friends, 35; How to Make Decisions About Things, 32; Appreciating the Best in—Radio, T.V., Movies, Comics, 31; Boy-Girl Relations, 30; Understanding Myself, 29; Problems of School Life, 29; How to Know Right from Wrong, 28; More About the Bible, 28; What My Denomination Believes, 26; Hit Parade of Favorite Hymns, 26; How a Christian Spends His Money, 24; About American Indians and Missions, 24; How to Live with Parents, 24; Understanding Worship in Church, 19; Frank Facts About Sex, 17; Personal Problems (gossip, swearing, cheating, sportsmanship), 17; Personal Devotions and Prayer, 16; Clinic on Manners, 16; Do We Need Rules and Authority, 15.

Senior highs

Seniors are enlarging their mental horizons, especially if still in school. They are greatly in need of corresponding growth in their knowledge of the Bible, and of Christian standards for personal conduct and social adjustment. They may not be aware of this need, nor too eager to apply themselves to study. But the clever teacher knows how to spark the imagination. He puts temptations to growth in their path and nudges them at the right moment so that they discover for themselves the values in study of the Bible and other religious literature.

The denominational study-discussion units will help the counselor to choose the areas of study most meaningful to senior highers, and set clear-cut objectives for growth. At least two sessions each week are important. There are many needs, and many essential areas for study. The evening Fellowship meeting gives opportunity to review many problems for which there is not sufficient time in the morning Fellowship class.

Employed youth and students

Older youth are not necessarily fully equipped for life. If they are to find increasing satisfaction in their Christian experience, there must be growth in knowledge of the Christian way. The program may include many elective units or studies based upon texts of a broad nature. It is a good idea to fit them together into a balanced whole, and to deal with them in a logical order. Many older youth are resourceful enough to develop their own studies and to seek out their own resource materials. This is often true of student groups, or of individuals in the older youth group who have completed their college work. A bookshelf of source materials helps. Also frequent reference to the objectives of Christian education. Denominational study-discussion materials aid in providing a rounded study program, and in avoiding haphazard approaches.

MATERIALS FOR STUDY—THE CURRICULUM

For the most part, local churches will use the denominationally approved materials for the various sessions of the Fellowship. There is wisdom in doing this. The lesson courses are carefully prepared to conform to the distinctive heritage and belief of the denomination, to achieve balance in relation to the objectives of Christian education, and to build progressively on the foundations laid in earlier years.

For the Sunday morning session

The materials for use in the Sunday morning church school session of the Fellowship are essentially of three types: the *graded lessons,* the *elective units,* and the *uniform lessons.* These call for separate consideration.

Graded lessons are prepared, in addition to uniform lessons, by most denominations. They have been undergoing a constant process of improvement for many years in which there has been wide sharing of experience through the National Council of Churches.

The graded lessons have marked advantages: 1. They are designed with the purpose of including all the objectives of Christian education, and with the goal of producing a balanced Christian life. 2. They are able to make use of a large amount of biblical material because the scope of problems discussed in the different age groups permits a wide range of Scripture from all portions of the Bible. 3. The passages are selected to suit the understanding of pupils of different ages, and the utmost consideration is given to using the Bible meaningfully and vitally. 4. The aim is to make them life-centered in purpose, in harmony with educational practice, yet also Bible-centered and Christ-centered in content. 5. The intent is to emphasize spiritual results by bringing the pupil face to face with Christ, the church, and life choices at the most appropriate time in his life.

Graded lessons fall roughly into two categories: *closely graded* and *cycle* (or departmental) *graded*. A graded course for each age or school grade is provided by the closely graded lessons. In smaller churches, with two or more ages or grades represented in one class, the closely graded lessons are taught in rotation over a span of several years. The cycle graded lessons are graded by departments, covering a span of three years, all pupils in the department using the same lesson. After the three years, there is another cycle, and so on.

Certain denominations have developed what has been called a *unified curriculum*. An emphasis is selected for a year, or for a quarter, and all the courses for the different grades throughout the church school are in this field of emphasis. It is felt that this approach to curriculum will help to unite the church in worship themes and activity projects, and to bring families closer together in Christian education.

As *elective units* carry no date, they may be used at any time as alternate materials. Through the elective principle, it is felt that a somewhat more tailor-made program may be developed to meet special needs and interests. This principle is believed to be well suited to older youth, whether employed or students, where interests tend to vary widely, and to have merit also for senior and junior highs. An interest finder, or check sheet, is of help in determining priority of need and assuring comprehensiveness.

Uniform lessons have been in existence for many decades. They are designed with the goal of giving a fairly comprehensive grasp of the Bible in a span of several years, through a cycle of Bible lessons developed by a central lesson committee of the National Council of Churches. In this system a passage of Scripture is made the organizing center of each lesson.

The uniform lessons have certain advantages: 1. They seek to make direct approach to the Bible. 2. They aim to give a working knowledge of the contents of the Bible. 3. They attempt to apply biblical teaching directly to life. 4. They seek to major on biblical passages suitable to simultaneous use by a wide span of ages. 5. A large assortment of helps is available from many sources.

For the evening meeting

The evening Fellowship meeting material also varies widely in different denominations and with different age groups. Monthly or quarterly magazines, annual program kits, and various study-discussion units are published. Program materials usually include various patterns for the meetings, discussion suggestions, and action projects. Correlation with the study materials for the Fellowship morning class session is generally on a broad basis, providing supplemental or parallel themes and, often, shorter discussion units or one-session topics.

Supplemental materials and resources

In addition to the prescribed or regular curriculum, there are many supplemental study materials. Some of these fall into broad classifications, such as those for the vacation church school, for the weekday church school, for the summer camps, for the annual missionary education study themes, for

---

HOW TO USE STUDY-DISCUSSION RESOURCES

1. Discover actual needs of your own group—use an interest finder.

2. Review denominational printed materials, audio-visuals, and other resources—consider needs and helps for the various Fellowship sessions.

3. Co-operate with your local church board of Christian education in selecting and using regular materials.

4. Use resources creatively: (a) adapt to your own group; (b) enlist wide participation, encourage originality; (c) supplement with your own ideas and additional aids.

5. Correlate supplemental resources: (a) build up your library and resource files; (b) use the *Audio-Visual Resource Guide* of the National Council of Churches, and catalogues of denominational publications; (c) relate resource persons and materials to your study-discussion units, central themes and objectives; (d) provide for advance preparation and for follow-up.

---

the weekday club groups, and those on special themes such as stewardship, evangelism, personal devotions, friendship and marriage, vocation, social problems, the church, the Bible, Christian beliefs, and leadership training.

For the eager minds of junior highs, some of them with omnivorous reading habits, there are many books and booklets for reading and study, written on their level of maturity. These provide insight concerning the Bible, and with regard to personalities, events, achievements, the Christian mission, vocations, hobbies, skills, and interests. For seniors, with expanding knowledge and interest, there are many supplemental resources for study in the fields just mentioned and others. For students and employed youth, the available resources are vast, and increasing constantly. A bookcase, or better yet, a branch or a section of the church library, is an indispensable aid. A few books added each year, or each month, rapidly become a nucleus for a study center. Attractive booklets and manuals should be included. The denominational bookstore catalogues and national religious education magazines should be checked frequently to locate new titles. The minister should be consulted; also, regional or national offices of the denominational educational, social progress, and missionary departments; and the area offices of the Council of Churches.

VARIED WAYS OF MAKING STUDY EFFECTIVE

Reliving experience through stories and illustrations

Good stories recreate real life, and stimulate the listeners to think, to discuss, and to identify themselves with possible answers to the problems raised. Stories illustrate and vitalize the truth, make clear the unfamiliar, develop spiritual sensitivity, encourage Christian choices, and save costly errors through vicarious experience. A story may be used as an entire lesson, to introduce discussion, to present a brief sketch or episode, or to climax discussion. From many, many sources good stories are available — the Bible, fiction, biographies, missionary achievement, incidents in history, magazines and newspapers, and everyday life.

Stimulating discussion

Using questions. One of the highest skills for the teacher-leader to cultivate is the effective use of questions — to provoke thought, to stimulate healthy emotional and intellectual participation, to solve problems. This is one way of talking things over in a friendly but vigorous fashion, of checking and double checking facts and opinions, of considering alternatives, and reaching agreement.

The life-situation or problem approach. Through real life situations and actual problems of a truly representative nature, young people are helped to anticipate experience. The Bible deals with many such situations. Jesus revealed his amazing skill as a teacher in his ability to deal spontaneously with real situations as they arose, and to create, through his parables and in other ways, imaginary situations which had real meaning to his listeners. The pressing problems of youth today may be presented through narrative sketches, multiple-choice considerations, "what-would-you-do" episodes, or audio-visual portrayals.

The use of panels and interviews. One of the advantages of the discussion method in making study effective is that it lends itself to many stimulating ways of enlisting participation. Among these are the panel in its various forms, the symposium, the dialogue, trialogue or interview, the open forum, round table, or question period. Young people and adult leaders should be encouraged to experiment with various techniques of this type in order to get the benefit of experienced resource persons, and to improve the process of group thinking and participation.

Group dynamics

In many ways the approach known as "group dynamics" offers great assistance to the goal of achieving Christian solidarity or "groupness." It seeks to treat each person as a respected and wanted member, with a mission to perform. It seeks to have each person share in group thinking, planning, and action. Thus the living church as "a dwelling place of God in the Spirit" (Eph. 2:22) is revealed in miniature in a

Christian Youth Fellowship in which all feel themselves to be "no longer strangers . . . but . . . members of the household of God . . ." (Eph. 2:19).

Leadership shifts from one to another — president, adviser, committee chairman, leader of the meeting, teacher, member of the group — and all feel they are a vital part and share responsibility.

In a practical sense the hunger for friends to "pal around with," the sense of belonging to a "gang," the fun of "taking our hair down" and "talking things over in a bull session," the thrill of "doing something together that counts" — all these are given solid strength through the procedures of group dynamics, which reveal how and why people interract upon one another. Group dynamics are not just a series of devices or clever tricks to manipulate people or to expedite study, discussion and action. They strike much deeper. Emotional blocks, disinterestedness, aggressive or withdrawal behavior, are replaced by trust in one another, by the application of the Golden Rule in the spirit of love and faith, and therefore by sound intellectual and emotional involvement.

Buzz sessions or discussion huddles. This technique for making the discussion method more dynamic in spirit has been widely used by junior and senior highs as well as by older youth and adults. It involves dividing the Youth Fellowship meeting, departmental session, or class into small "buzz groups" or "huddles" (approximately six persons) for brief discussion (approximately six to ten minutes) of a specific question or problem. Usually a spokesman is named, and each person in turn is asked to offer suggestions, which are summarized and reported when the entire group convenes.

Role-playing. This is a form of spontaneous drama in which parts or roles are informally played, usually without rehearsal, by members selected from the group to portray the reactions of certain types of persons to a particular situation. The problem-situation must be one which is real to the group, though not experienced in its exact form by the group (to avoid attempts to imitate actual events). To avoid embarrassment, it is made clear that the actors do not play themselves. Thus the dynamic qualities in the situation — the struggles, tensions, and feelings — may be shared freely by actors and audience without arousing defensive emotions. An essential element in role-playing is the period of analysis and evaluation which follows — usually involving an appraisal of the accuracy with which the assigned roles were played and of the reasons why the actors reacted as they did.

In group dynamics it is essential for all to become interested in improving the group process and the group spirit. Openheartedness, freedom, and honesty are emphasized as over against aggressiveness, rigidity, defensiveness.

Audio-visuals

Another valuable way of making study effective is through audio-visuals. These help to make abstract truth concrete, to stir the emotions, and to assist action. They include flat pictures, concrete objects, recordings and colored slides (with or without sound), as well as motion pictures.

Effective use requires good equipment, suitable surroundings, and proficient operators (see *The Audio-Visual Projectionist's Handbook*). There should be understanding of the educational and spiritual objectives, correlation with other aids and plans in teaching, preparation of the group for the showing, and, frequently, follow-up plans. For suggestions see denominational publications and the *Audio-Visual Resource Guide for Use in Christian Education*. The *Youth Audio-Visual Kit* is a useful aid in strengthening the understanding of the Fellowship and its functioning.

Chapter VIII

THE FELLOWSHIP IN ACTION

"Be doers of the word, and not hearers only . . ." [1]

The inspiration for all Christian action is in the life and teaching of him who "went about doing good" and who said, "I am among you as one who serves." The objective of every Youth Fellowship at this point is expressed thus in the Scriptures: "Through love be servants of one another. For the whole law is fulfilled in one word, 'You shall love your neighbor as yourself' " (Gal. 5:13-14).

CHRISTIAN YOUTH MUST ACT

"Let's do something to show we mean what we say," said a high school girl in a meeting on "To Be Christian Is to Share."

"How about gathering clothing for Europe on Halloween instead of the usual party — sort of a glorified trick or treat," suggested the leader. He had picked this idea up in a magazine.

"We could invite the other youth groups of our church and of the neighborhood to join us," someone added. And in no time at all the plans were laid. The college age as well as the junior and senior highers joined in. The result — a chain of meaningful action — a mound of clothing shipped to needy people, a Halloween party with a new spirit, community co-operation, a fuller appreciation of one aspect of the Christian life.

"Let's get some action on this TV business, if we really want to know what our TV score is and how to improve it,"

[1] James 1:22.

suggested a junior high adviser. "How'd you like to take a TV poll to find out what's really going on?" This led to a most interesting project. Assignments were made to cover various channels, neighbors were interviewed, questionnaires were submitted to the junior highs, a parents' night was set up with a panel of parents and junior highs, a report was submitted on the poll and there was much discussion.

Such incidents remind us that there is a divine commission laid upon every Christian, just because he is a Christian, to act his faith. This is inherent in being a true disciple of him whose teaching was never empty theory, but was always joined to action. His teachings were summons to action — "Go . . . teach," "This do," "Go and do likewise." His life was and is the greatest challenge to action in all history. Action is characteristic of youth, because of pressures within which drive them to experiment, to explore, to express themselves.

WHAT KIND OF ACTION?

There is a special quality or spirit in Christian action. It differs widely from mere self-expression. To prod church youth into being active just for the sake of keeping them busy is a dangerous thing. The church should not make the mistake of carrying the limitations and inadequacies of secularism over into the field of religion. There is futility in going through the motions without discovery of meaning. There is danger in filling the lives of energetic junior and senior highers and older youth with a clutter of meetings, parties, and projects without worthy motives. That is why some young people think they have "gone stale" on the church. They have missed the real thing.

The motivation of Christian action is not self-centeredness, its spirit is not condescending paternalism; it expresses genuine Christianity. Christian service is Christlike in that it is compassionate, loving, and unselfish. It arises out of a real concern for human personality and a desire to do the will of God. It is action with a purpose, intelligently conceived and executed, persistently undertaken with a spirit of abandon, in faith believing that the Christian can do "all things through Christ." Of course not all church activity reaches these ideal levels, yet the aim should be to get as near to them as possible. When Christianity is really tried in undiluted form it produces unbelievable results. This is the spirit which should characterize the Youth Fellowship in a time like this.

THE VALUE AND FUNCTION OF PROJECTS

A project may be described as an undertaking directed toward a worth-while goal, involving planning, the execution of logical steps, and a sense of tangible achievement. Projects vary in type — study, worship, recreation, service. Often, though not always, there is a goal of expressing Christian ideals in some helpful way beyond the groups. Not all ideas for action mentioned in this chapter and the next may be regarded as projects.

Christian service should go on from day to day in many unorganized ways which express the spirit of the Master in deeds of helpfulness. There are a number of good reasons, however, for establishing projects:

1. They dramatize areas of Christian action so as to stimulate imagination and sustain interest.

2. They make possible greater achievement by increasing the number and scope of tangible things done.

3. They encourage wider co-operation and group effort.

4. They permit better "calendaring" and timing, and leave less to chance.

5. They train young people in orderly planning and in systematic check-up.

TEST OF A GOOD PROJECT

1. Does it sound exciting—and challenging?
2. Does it have a worth-while purpose?
3. Does it stimulate creativity?
4. Is it suited to age-group capacities and interests?
5. Does it encourage wide participation?
6. Is it well timed?

THE FIVE AREAS OF EMPHASIS AND ACTION

The five areas of emphasis which we have previously discussed in terms of planning, structure, worship, and study have great value in organizing and co-ordinating the action program. If the year's calendar includes provision for several action projects related to each of the five areas, there is good assurance of a year of balanced accomplishment. If the Youth Fellowship is organized with separate committees or commissions for each of the areas, the chairmen with their groups have the responsibility for initiating and carrying through general ideas for action and specific action projects. This means that more people are put to work, and that each project gets its full measure of attention. Junior high groups, for whom standing committees are not recommended, may preserve this same balance by selecting projects from the five areas and assigning them to short-term committees.

Examples of representative ideas for action and specific action projects for each of the five areas are given below. Many ideas are included in order to offer tangible helps to guide leaders and to stimulate varied programs and plans. This is not intended as a complete list — in fact, it is important that each group use its own originality in creating ideas and projects which fit its own needs, and learn to follow its own judgment and interests in the choice of projects.

Some projects fit junior highs best; others, older youth; some are suitable for combined action by two or more age groups. Since junior high interests change quickly, their leaders should help them to select good short-term projects. Some projects are challenging enough to justify repetition from year to year or on a two- or three-year cycle; others are of a "once-for-all" nature. Ideas for general action may be simple or quite elaborate, may involve one session or one week, or may be spread over many months. Projects likewise vary in amount of time and effort required, in their appeal to the group, and in the results achieved. The adult leader should help his group to consider these factors carefully when plans are made. The action areas of the Youth Fellowship program — *Faith, Witness, Outreach, Citizenship, Fellowship* — are all interrelated, and hence may overlap. Each has qualities of distinctness which lead naturally into definite types of action. Each of these areas is the concern of all in the Youth Fellowship, yet responsibility for taking initiative in worship, study, and action for each area may well be placed upon one person in a small church, or several persons in a large church.

1. Christian Faith — Ideas for Action

It should be borne in mind that study and worship are actually forms of action, and that many projects are possible involving worship or study, or both. Furthermore, the concept of faith which we have been discussing in this book is one which expresses itself in action. The Book of James indicates that "faith by itself, if it has no works, is dead" (James 2:17).

Although faith is personal and intimate, it is also something to be shared with others; though it involves beliefs to be accepted, it also is a way of life to be expressed; though it assumes a feeling of confidence and sureness, it also must be alive and growing, a dynamic force manifesting itself in every human relationship and supremely in fellowship with God. Faith, first of all, is *an attitude, a way of feeling* — that of *trust*. Next, it is *a body of beliefs, a way of thinking* — not isolated convictions, separate and distinct from each other, but a unified philosophy of life, referred to as "the Christian faith," which is centered in the fact of God as revealed in Christ. Finally, it is *an approach to daily existence, a way of living* — the life of faith. Jesus said, "According to your faith be it done to you" (Matt. 9:29), and again, "If you have faith . . . nothing will be impossible to you" (Matt. 17:20).

The source of faith is God — on every hand we are confronted with him and are impelled to respond to his love and to do his will. The foundation of faith is an *experience* of Jesus Christ as Savior and Lord, as Friend and Companion. He is "the pioneer and perfecter of our faith" (Heb. 12:2). Upon this foundation must be built a solid structure.

With respect to the area of Faith, here are some ideas and suggestions for action.

Understanding the Christian faith

— Use the regular denominational lesson materials and study-discussion units, emphasizing the topics or units which deal with Christian beliefs, the Christian heritage, denominational beliefs and heritage.

— Develop a statement of Christian faith of your own, following such a study.

— Hold a forum or a series of forums on Christian beliefs, using the minister, the adult adviser, or an outside speaker, and dividing into buzz groups.

— Arrange a special study course on Christian beliefs or on the Christian heritage, using supplemental study material.

— Develop a bookshelf of significant books on Christian theology and heritage especially suitable for young people.

— Study the progress of the church in the early Christian centuries, the Reformation and its leaders, the development of the missionary movement and the achievements of its pioneers.

— Plan a historical exhibit covering old pictures, costumes, Bibles, records. Write a newspaper, or prepare and produce a skit. Make display posters covering historical data. Include material about your own church. Compile a scrapbook for permanent use to present to your church. Take pictures or colored slides of your church, its activities and groups.

— Ask your minister to preach sermons on such themes as "Beliefs that Matter" and "A Faith for Youth to Live By."

— Co-operate with your minister in encouraging classes on the meaning of church membership.

— Prepare a *Who's Who in Church History*, including pictures or names of prominent leaders, facts about their lives and significance. Also try this idea for *Who's Who in Missions* or *Who's Who in My Denomination*.

— Appoint "reporters" to interview ministers of other denominations, or to dig up facts in the library concerning the background, beliefs, and heritage of the various denominations.

Personal commitment and conduct

— Provide opportunities in co-operation with the minister for the registry of commitment to Christ and the decision to join the church.

— Utilize seasonal moods and special occasions, as Christmas, Easter, New Year's, Thanksgiving, for services of dedication or commitment, candlelight services, campfires.

— Build plans for a "New Friends for Christ Weekend," a house party or retreat, a winter, spring, or summer camp, Declaration Sunday, a Day of Renewal, Forward Step Sunday, or Youth Week, so as to encourage meaningful spiritual commitments.

— Plan a Youth Fellowship evangelistic project.

— Develop a "Discipleship Covenant" or "Rule for Christian Living" as a result of study and discussion. (See biblical references to covenant; i.e., Genesis 15:1-21; Exodus 4:24-26; 24:8; Deuteronomy 5:2-3, and note various church and Youth Fellowship covenants or formulations of spiritual disciplines.) Have various members of the Christian Faith commission or of the entire Youth Fellowship propose wordings for specific items.

— Plan a series of meetings, using life-situation dramas, role-playing, audio-visuals, or panel discussions, to consider Christian standards of personal conduct.

Personal enrichment and growth

— Encourage daily personal devotions by each member of the Fellowship, offering suggestions about regular helps.

— Promote a Bible-reading program, using a reading schedule and other helps. (Write to denominational headquarters or the American Bible Society, 450 Park Ave., New York 22, N. Y.)

— Emphasize the Bible study units in the Sunday morning and evening sessions of the Fellowship.

— Start a Fellowship Cell group or an "Order of the Yoke" for Bible study, prayer and personal sharing. (See *Spiritual Power Through Fellowship Cells*, United Christian Youth Movement.)

— Develop Bible quizzes, Bible time-line or ladder, scrapbooks, relief maps, and other projects as suggested in the regular curriculum.

— Train a verse-speaking choir, with light and dark voices, in the use of the Bible, poetry, and other devotional material in worship services.

— Encourage participation in church services of worship and in the weekly church prayer meeting.

— Train younger and older youth in the planning and conducting of worship services and devotional meetings of many types.

— Develop a file of worship and devotional materials—hymns, poetry quotations, pictures, stories, litanies, etc.

— Hold a "fix-things-up" or "beautification" project each year to improve the appearance and equipment of the Youth Fellowship rooms.

— Expand the Youth Fellowship bookshelf or library with books on the Bible, prayer, biography, worship, and containing worship resources.

2. CHRISTIAN WITNESS — IDEAS FOR ACTION

Inherent in the very nature of the Christian faith is the necessity of sharing it with others by example and by spoken word. "Witnessing is something that we carry on all the time — by our lives, by the use of our money, by our activities in church, by the use of our leisure time, and by Christian living in our daily vocations. It is the things that we do, together with the things that we say . . ." [2] Witnessing is thus the concern of every Christian.

[2] From *Handbook: Senior High Fellowship*. Copyright, 1952. John Knox Press. Used by permission.

THE FELLOWSHIP IN ACTION

Evangelism

— Develop a "responsibility list" of prospects for the Youth Fellowship and for church membership. Conduct a community canvass, if necessary, check names of school friends, job associates, club members, neighbors, new arrivals in town; co-operate in an interdenominational use of religious preference cards.

— Conduct a "New Friends for Christ Program," a Youth Evangelism Weekend, a "Christian Witness Mission," a "Win My Friend Week," or a "Youth Friendly Month."

— Hold an evangelism study class, a "Christian Witness Workshop," a Youth to Youth Evangelism Clinic to help train young people for witnessing.

— Co-operate with other churches in a Mission to High School Students, a Religious Emphasis Week (college students), or a United Christian Youth Mission.

Stewardship

— Emphasize study-discussion units in the regular curriculum, or in supplemental material on stewardship.

— Take a "Time Survey" of your Youth Fellowship members and help each to build a Christian "Time Budget."

— Make an inventory of abilities, talents, and skills represented in your Fellowship.

— Hold a stewardship speaking contest, an essay contest, or a poster contest.

— Co-operate in a Youth budget with emphasis upon proportionate giving. Conduct an every-member canvass of youth by youth.

— Conduct an every-member enlistment-for-service program, using sign-up cards or blanks.

Churchmanship

— Hold "Churchmanship Quizzes," "Churchmanship Clinics," or "Churchmanship Workshops," to study ways in which to be more effective church members.

— Study and discuss topics on the church and its beliefs—its heritage —its redemptive task—its activities—its worship services—its social action program—its world mission—its ordinances and practices—its educational program.

151

— Emphasize regular church attendance and service.

— Conduct a "Church Loyalty Crusade," using record cards to check attendance at church, morning and evening youth meetings, Bible reading, prayer, systematic giving.

— Appoint youth sponsors to integrate new members and visitors into the life of the church.

— Hold a "Fix-Things-Up Party," "Paint-Pot Party," or "Clean-up Campaign" to help beautify and improve the church or its children's or youth rooms.

— Arrange to have young people serve on church committees and boards. Study the church's program and recommend advance steps through them.

Vocation

— Emphasize study-discussion units on vocation.

— Develop and expand your Youth Fellowship vocations bookshelf and pamphlets.

— Conduct a Vocations Conference or Career Clinic with the help of resource leaders or specialists in vocational guidance.

— Arrange vocational interviews on various occupations.

— Provide vocational aptitude tests, personality profiles and personal counseling through professionally qualified leaders with Christian insight.

— Conduct vocational excursions or tours to furnish insight concerning factories, hospitals, courtrooms, stores, farms, offices, colleges, etc.

— Secure and review catalogues and other literature from church colleges.

3. CHRISTIAN OUTREACH — IDEAS FOR ACTION

The Christian church has a world mission in which every Christian shares — to make Christ known to all peoples everywhere, to produce disciples committed to him, and to provide churches expressing his spirit in all human relationships. This mission begins close at hand and reaches to the ends of the earth.

Home and foreign missions

— Use missionary units in the regular curriculum, adding current materials.

— Expand each year your shelf of missionary books. Promote a reading program.

— Help sponsor a School of Missions or a School of World Friendship.

— Make missionary maps (relief maps, electric maps, etc.) .

— Establish a missionary current events bulletin board. Highlight such events regularly in youth meetings. Appoint "commentators."

— Start and maintain a world outreach file—biographical sketches, stories, poems, prayers, litanies, hymns, Scripture.

— Use missionary audio-visuals. (See *Audio-Visual Resource Guide*.)

— Produce missionary plays or episodes. Try role-playing a problem situation.

— Write to pen pals or to mission fields.

— Assist in white cross work (boxes of requested materials for missionaries) . Discover and fill needs for books, magazines, pictures, Christmas cards, paints, and brushes, bandages, supplies, clothing, food.

— Co-operate with the Christian Fellowship commission in nationality "fun and festival parties," using appropriate food, decorations, games.

— Sponsor a "The World in Our Town" missionary exhibit and folk festival, with booths for various countries supplied by church school classes and departments.

— Develop plans to increase youth missionary giving (Youth Budget) .

— Make a missionary curio case or costume chest.

— Solicit and prepare volunteers for help in Christian centers, summer service projects, and work camps; to serve as missionary interns.

— Start an "adventure in friendship" or "get-acquainted project"— exchange letters, pictures, and "appreciation objects" with nationality groups in America or overseas; arrange a "hospitality weekend" with foreign students; exchange visits with racial and nationality groups.

The ecumenical movement

— Appoint "investigators" to bring reports of "religious current events" regarding agencies and activities in "co-operative Christianity."

— Co-operate in the annual community and national observance of Youth Week, sponsored by the United Christian Youth Movement.

— Sponsor a "united front" interchurch Christian youth radio or TV program.

— Use "World Communion Sunday" (first Sunday in October) and "World Day of Prayer" (first Friday in Lent) to emphasize the ecumenical movement.

— Co-operate in an ecumenical work camp. (Write to the Youth Department, National Council of Churches, 120 E. 23rd St., New York 10, N. Y., for detailed information.)

— Co-operate with your community Christian Youth Council in interchurch events and projects. Help start a council if none exists.

Overseas relief and reconstruction

— Investigate and support current projects of Church World Service and of denominational and general agencies, such as CARE, Meals for Millions, Heifers for Relief.

— Use originality in developing ways to keep your Youth Fellowship informed about needs, and to collect clothing, blankets, medicine, tools, supplies, and money.

— Plan a Thanksgiving, Christmastime, or Good Friday sacrificial meal and service.

Peace and world order

— Observe United Nations Day (October 24). This may be extended to a week. Present facts about UN and its achievements. Put on a simplified session of UN, using placards, flags, "delegates," charts, etc.

— Hold an "Open House to the World." (See UCYM manual on this subject, including plans for formulating a "Bill of Human Rights" in a city-wide institute.)

— Conduct an opinion poll of young people and adults on world order issues.

— Set up a peace bulletin board and literature rack.

— Conduct international relations workshops or world peace study groups.

— Engage in a Hospitality Weekend, entertaining overseas students in homes.

— Encourage letter-writing campaigns when issues warrant.

— Make a United Nations stamp collection, including data concerning countries represented (a good junior high project).

— Develop specific plans to study and co-operate with International Refugee Organization; World Health Organization; United Nation International Children's Emergency Fund; United Nations Educational, Scientific, and Cultural Organization.

— Develop "appreciation evenings" involving nationality fun and festival ideas, folk songs, art, music, literature, games, costumes, food.

— Promote exchange letters, pictures, objects of interest. Encourage exchange visits, exchange students, and world travel and travelogues.

— Formulate a "World Good Neighbor Policy" to express Christian ideals.

4. CHRISTIAN CITIZENSHIP — IDEAS FOR ACTION

The Christian is both a citizen in the kingdom of God and in his own country. The gospel of Christ compels him to go the second mile in serving the needs of others. He is under obligation to change unchristian conditions in society and to promote justice in all human relationships.

Service to the local church

— Help maintain and beautify your church building and grounds.

— Repaint, repair, or create equipment for use in children's or youth departments—chairs, tables, cabinets, bookcases, chalk boards, drapes, bulletin boards, etc.

— Assist in mimeographing, poster-making, typing, mailing, telephoning, filing, transportation, visitation.

— Help in the educational program—with children, in the nursery, with club groups.

— Furnish helpers for the church library—cataloguing, repairing books, etc.

— Assist in the serving of meals, ushering, collecting and placing magazines, etc.

— Help in a vacation church school or day camp for your own church or in some other rural or city community.

Community service

— Assist in helpful ministries to hospitals, prisons, homes; to underprivileged or neglected persons, the aged, the blind, newcomers in town, etc.

— Furnish volunteer assistance to social service and community welfare organizations. Study conditions, propose remedies and help establish them.

— Provide help to special groups—migrants, servicemen and servicewomen, nationality groups.

— Sponsor or assist in weekend work camps (rural or city).

— Start a mission or assist in one already established—furnish teachers, club leaders, materials, or work-camp crew.

— Launch a community clean-up and beautification campaign—plant trees, clear vacant lots for playgrounds, remove trash.

— Collect materials (clothing, food, furniture, toys, books, magazines) for social agencies—Salvation Army, Goodwill Industries, Church World Service.

Intergroup relations and social problems

— Sponsor plays, audio-visuals and other programs.

— Study biographies, beliefs, architecture, symbols, achievements, practices.

— Co-operate with other groups in projects to meet community needs.

— Plan an intercultural festival or entertainment for Brotherhood Week in February.

— Arrange field trips, seminars and panels to study labor unions, housing and health conditions, educational opportunities, unemployment, co-operatives, courts.

— Hold political education seminars for new voters.

— Work for improved legislation and the preservation of civil liberties.

— Survey facts concerning social problems (see list above) —develop plans for improvement.

5. CHRISTIAN FELLOWSHIP — IDEAS FOR ACTION

These ideas are developed in Chapter IX on "The Fellowship at Play."

SOURCES FOR IDEAS AND INFORMATION

Much of the success of the Youth Fellowship depends upon the attractiveness and appeal of the action projects it undertakes, and upon the feeling that important things are happening. It is of great value to exercise resourcefulness in discovering workable projects. There are a number of good sources for ideas:

1. *Denominational youth action manuals.* Each group should start with its own denominational material. Some de-

nominations publish separate manuals for the five areas of action, others combine them in one handbook. Most denominations have separate materials for junior highs. An excellent plan is to build a bookshelf of resource materials on activities, including the manuals of other denominations.

2. *Denominational magazines and story papers.* These publications contain many interesting articles on current action projects of youth groups, often with a seasonal emphasis or tie-up. These magazines should be filed with notations for future reference.

3. *Interdenominational materials.* The youth materials of the National Council of Churches offer many ideas for youth action projects — for example, Youth Week, Family Week, Christian Education Week. Many of these may be undertaken co-operatively on an interchurch, or community basis; for example, a Youth evangelism project. In some fields of specialized interest, such as evangelism, missions, student work, junior high work, stewardship, audio-visuals, social action, relief, there are denominational or interdenominational departments from which suggestions for study and action may be secured. In other fields, such as United Nations, world order, vocation, labor, employment, housing, delinquency, there are reliable sources for information which should be known and used.

4. *Camps, conferences, coaching clinics.* One reason for sending young people — both officers and members — to area conferences, leadership training classes, summer camps, and coaching clinics is so that they may swap ideas with young people and leaders from other churches and come back loaded with suggestions. Junior highs and younger seniors attending camps and conferences gain ideas from the varied programs, projects, interest groups, and general activities which they can help put to work "back home."

CHAPTER IX

THE FELLOWSHIP AT PLAY

"Let us rejoice and be glad . . ." [1]

THE TRUE MEANING OF CHRISTIAN FELLOWSHIP

A revolutionary concept lies at the center of the church youth program — love for others. The Christian approach to fellowship is different and distinctive. Friendliness is at the very heart of the Christian gospel. But much more is involved than merely "winning friends and influencing people" (for selfish purposes). The quality of personal concern — genuine interest in the welfare of others — is involved. Jesus said, "By this all men will know that you are my disciples, if you have love for one another" (John 13:35). In the Youth Fellowship this spirit of outward-going love (the New Testament *agape*) expresses itself day after day in many little ways toward the friendless and least popular. The true Christian seeks to go below the surface to understand sympathetically why a person is timid, or feels inferior, or acts in an unpleasant or overly aggressive manner. Even more, he seeks to do something to reveal his genuine interest and to create friendliness. Can this ideal goal be achieved? The Youth Fellowship movement is based upon the faith that it can be — in the Christian church.

FELLOWSHIP IN PERSONAL RELATIONSHIPS

The high ideal of true Christian fellowship expresses itself first toward God and then toward others in the personal relationships of two or more individuals. Jesus said, "You shall love . . . God . . . and . . . your neighbor as yourself." Can

[1] Psalm 118:24.

the Youth Fellowship be so filled with the spirit of Christ that each member — or at least the majority — will seek out others in the group and outside the group with whom to share Christian ideals and experiences? Can the youth organization become a truly *redemptive fellowship* in which the dominant spirit is that of helping each person to become his best? Can the experiences of play, recreation, and enjoyment be such that everyone, without exception, has a grand good time and feels himself to be fully accepted as a part of the group? These are vital questions — much more important than those applying to smooth functioning of program and statistical "success." They have been and can be answered in the affirmative. Here is another area for applying Christian faith with venturesomeness and enthusiasm.

CHRISTIAN FELLOWSHIP CHECK SHEET
(Score a maximum of ten for each point)

How Do We Rate as a *Christian* Fellowship?

1. When a new person visits our group, is he or she treated coolly and held at arm's length, or made a part of the group?

2. Are we satisfied to let our crowd remain much as it is, quite indifferent to others, or do we actively seek out others and draw them into our Fellowship?

3. If two, three or four young people are particularly good friends, do they build psychological walls around their friendship until they become a clique, or do they continually seek to enlarge their circle?

4. If a boy and a girl are "that way" about each other, do they practically monopolize each other, or does each of them take an interest in others of *both* sexes?

5. When younger ones graduate into an older group, are they singled out by the older ones for personal friendship and quickly made a part of the group?

6. Are the less attractive and intelligent made to feel at ease at parties, in discussions, in group conversations?

7. Are those who run with a "fast crowd" outside the church, or whose

standards are otherwise low, helped through friendship to set Christian ideals and to find personal fulfillment in the church gang or group?

8. Are committee responsibilities passed around, and the less capable helped to grow?

9. Do our Youth Fellowship members have friends of one racial, national, or cultural background only, or do they, as followers of Christ, seek friends of all backgrounds and take steps to encourage interracial and intercultural acquaintances, joint activity and membership?

10. Is a feeling of group solidarity and "Christian community" built up so that the church Youth Fellowship is actually the strongest center of interest and loyalty for all its members and a vital force to attract others?

FELLOWSHIP IN GROUP ACTIVITY

Play while you work

Literally, Christian work can be fun, and young people can enjoy Christian service. One of the country's best-known preachers once said, "I get more fun out of preparing sermons than anything else I do, yet it is extremely hard work." The young people of the author's own church have discovered how much fun they can find in hard manual work. Each year for several years he and they have put on old clothes, assembled paintbrushes and tools, and spent long hours in Washington's Birthday holiday "Work Camp" or a Saturday "Paint Pot Party," beautifying some portion of the church or its equipment, only to discover an eagerness for more occasions of this type.

Working side by side in manual labor promotes conversation and stimulates fellowship. Co-operation in a work project which requires teamwork develops a sense of comradeship, mutual respect, and appreciation. This is part of the explanation of the popularity of barn raisings and husking bees. It is part of the philosophy underlying work camps and summer service projects.

Fun comes into such ventures at several points: first and

160

foremost, in the fun of accomplishment—the satisfaction in seeing something tangible completed; second, in the fun of fellowship — conversation, laughter, and pranks associated with the task; third, in the fun-features deliberately injected into the experience, concurrently with the work, interspersed at rest intervals, or after the work is done — games, singing, entertainment, and so forth. The leader who understands the deep-seated urge for self-expression and for social acceptance and approval which exists in every normal person is better equipped to understand so-called "horseplay" among junior highs and seniors and to keep it from getting out of hand and "spoiling the fun of the work." Such a leader stimulates individual achievement, encourages group acceptance of each individual, and constructive group pressure toward the purposes for which all are working.

Enjoying religion

Christianity was meant to be enjoyed — not in a superficial sense, but in ways deep and profound. That is why the Bible is so full of references to joy and gladness.

This sense of joy should be experienced in worship: "I was glad when they said to me, 'Let us go to the house of the Lord!'" (Ps. 122:1). "Make a joyful noise to God, all the earth; sing the glory of his name; give to him glorious praise!" (Ps. 66:1). Added joy is experienced when we are conscious of the presence of others in the fellowship of worship.

This sense of joy should also be expressed in service. He who has learned to "serve the Lord with gladness" (Ps. 100:2) has experienced one of the most satisfying of all the activities of life. Young people should be given the opportunity to know this joy and to share it in group activities of service. The Christian spirit of outgoing love and understanding thus finds expression in tangible acts of helpfulness.

Even in the midst of suffering, hardship, and opposition there may be this sense of deeper joy. The grim effects of human weakness and the stern realities of life serve but to make the true Christian more aware of the glorious fact of his redemption in Christ and the triumphant nature of his faith in the living God.

Fellowship singing

One of the most natural ways of expressing Christian fellowship is in group singing. This aspect of the church youth program is unusually popular and distinctive. It is most appropriate that the young people of the community should be able to look forward to a time every week, usually Sunday when they can enjoy a good hymn sing. Young people can have fun together singing many types of songs. They may deeply enjoy *great hymns*. They may find fresh meaning and strength in the simple but profound music and words of *spirituals*. They may find insight and international appreciation in *folk songs* from many lands. They may share wholesome sentiment and find real enjoyment in *popular songs* and *ballads*. They may find excitement in well-known *college* and *high school songs*, or laughter and fellowship in *fun songs*.

The choice of material for singing should be in keeping with the ideals and purposes of a Christian church. Fun songs should promote wholesome enjoyment and laughter but not through the use of coarse or vulgar ideas. Popular songs should be of a constructive type, with words and music consistent with Christian ideals, and without undue emphasis upon kissing and petting or upon ideas or conduct "unbecoming a Christian." Many folk songs which have won international favor, some having persisted for many decades, encourage fine sentiment and create appreciation of other peoples, customs, and places.

162

Fellowship in appreciation—music, drama, humor

Many fine channels are open to church youth groups when efforts are put forth to share appreciation and to find fellowship in varying experiences. One of the best of these is music. In addition to group singing, there are fine opportunities for fellowship in choir music, orchestras, vocal and instrumental numbers by soloists or by small or large groups. There are radio and TV programs, motion pictures with sound, and recordings. Some youth groups have found real response to the idea of "Music Appreciation Evenings" in homes or at the church, based upon the use of records.

Dramatics have had a significant place in the activities of many churches. Sanctuary dramas or pageants, worship dramas, plays, tableaux or skits — on many themes and suitable for varied occasions and purposes — are available. Doubtless much more use should be made by youth groups of drama in its simplest forms through episodes, spontaneous role-playing, Scripture-reading (with or without costumes), and play reading (in which parts are assigned and manuscripts are read, without stage properties or elaborate rehearsals). An increasing place is being assigned to high-quality motion pictures and other audio-visuals. The latter include film slide sets in color, covering the beauties of nature, reproductions of great religious paintings, and many other subjects. Now and then a theater party may be sponsored by the Youth Fellowship to witness some outstanding motion picture or play devoted to a biblical, historical, or other religious theme, or presenting great ideals, social problems, religious events or personalities (i.e., Martin Luther), or just offering good, wholesome entertainment. A large place should be made for humor and for clean fun of all sorts. Christian young people should learn that, ideally, the church should be "the best place in town to have a real good time."

THE FUNCTION OF PLAY

Relax and enjoy your religion

Just because Christianity is concerned about serious matters and about beliefs which people feel so keenly that they often become argumentative about them is no reason for the assumption that the normal attitude of a Christian is one of tension, worry, and anxiety. The reverse of this is true. The true Christian attitude is one of faith, which breeds confidence, poise, and power. Paul and Silas set the example when they sang Christian hymns while in prison. A "Singspiration" or a "Supersing" at a local "Fireside" or at an interchurch camp or convention may be a most natural expression of Christian joy. The love of play is not sacrilegious. The playful spirit in dealing with the relationships, tensions, and responsibilities of life is not flippancy but an instinctive expression of a God-given urge. Physical, mental, and spiritual good health spills over in laughter, and appreciates life. Under such circumstances, there is great enjoyment in religion. And more is accomplished. Quiet confidence replaces grimness, buoyant faith dissolves fatigue — life is at its best.

Improving oneself by play

Play has another function, an educational one. Some of the most necessary skills, the most valuable attitudes toward oneself and others, and the most desirable lessons in human relationships are learned through recreation. A well-rounded church-centered program of recreation will provide many opportunities for self-improvement — in physical co-ordination, teamwork, fair play, good sportsmanship; in mental alertness, social adjustment, friendliness; in developing techniques, talents, skills, and abilities.

Learning to live together

In many ways the most important lessons learned from play, from a Christian viewpoint, are those associated with learning to get along together in God's world. There is no better way to learn that we are brothers under the skin than by discovering that people from many different backgrounds, from various nations and races, laugh at the same jokes, enjoy the same games, admire the same character traits and skills.

CHRISTIAN FELLOWSHIP—IDEAS FOR ACTION

This, the fifth area of emphasis and action in the Youth Fellowship program, is broad in its scope and, like each of the others, needs careful organization and grouping of ideas and projects for action.

The church as a fellowship (local and interchurch)

— Promote friendliness among *all* young people—through discussions on the unselfish nature of true Christian friendship, through sharing informal occasions of fellowship, birthdays, achievements, disappointments.

— Make use of seasonal parties and holiday observances—Halloween, Thanksgiving, Christmas, New Year's Eve, Lincoln's Birthday and Washington's, Valentine's Day, St. Patrick's Day, April Fool's Day, Memorial Day, Fourth of July.

— Develop "traditions" of church-wide fellowship and service such as cheer-group trips to hospitals, homes, shut-ins; caroling; tape-recordings of church music and sermons to shut-ins.

— Set up service groups such as "work crew" or "clean-up-gang," "fix-it-shop"; repair broken furniture, rebind hymnals and library books, mow lawns, water plants, do mimeographing and other church office work, make posters, visit prospects, wash windows, clean floors, establish a baby-sitting service for church families.

— Share skills as ushers, musicians, greeters, hosts and hostesses; utilize leadership abilities as teachers, club leaders, vacation church school helpers, etc.

— Put spirit and creative ability into publicity, posters, study-discussion, worship, recreation, drama, music, and service projects of the Youth Fellowship.

— Make a survey of fellowship resources—rooms, equipment, agencies, leadership, community assets—and of the fellowship interests of the group as a basis for building a strong program.

— Help equip, decorate, and arrange the Youth Fellowship rooms to create an attractive and friendly atmosphere.

— Share fellowship in interchurch rallies, conferences, parties, outings, institutes, camps, caravans, service projects.

— Help form an interdenominational youth council and support cooperative projects, workshops, recreation, athletic leagues, TV and radio panels on youth theme, work camps, etc.

— Keep in touch with away-from-home young people in college, in the armed services, in out-of-town jobs. Mail personal letters, snapshots, round robins, news sheets, birthday and seasonal greetings. Send packages of candy, cookies, etc. Now and then have a "party" to write letters, make candy, cake, and cookies.

— Present going-away gifts to students, servicemen, and C.O.'s—Bibles, devotional books, religious pictures (for pocketbook or desk).

— Send letters of introduction to ministers, student advisers, chaplains.

— Arrange home-coming parties, reunions, and other get-togethers.

Boy-girl friendships

— Provide for study units and discussion meetings on boy-girl friendships, and on how to make more real friends.

— Provide opportunities for fellows and girls to be together in groups and as twosomes—parties, table games, game room, ping-pong, shuffleboard, outings, cook-outs, hikes, sleigh and hay rides, camping.

— Develop a boy-girl conduct code based upon the application of Christian ideals and including responsibilities to others in the Fellowship.

— Add suitable books and pamphlets to your church or Fellowship library after consulting the minister and other leaders for suggestions.

Christian home life

— Emphasize the family altar and other approaches to family worship —encourage the use of books of daily devotions and other devotional booklets suitable for young people. Suggest ways for youth to participate with others in the family.

— Provide plans and suggestions for family fun and outings—hikes trips, tours, games, riddles, puzzles, brain teasers, jokes, sings, records, radios, TV, gardening hobbies, birthdays, etc.

— Offer suggestions for interesting ways of observing holidays and using vacation periods.

— Stress reading books and magazines aloud with the family—and discussing current interests, religious topics, and world affairs.

— Suggest family projects—home repairs, workshop, painting, decorating; gardening (the Lord's Acre) ; securing Bible versions, hymnals, and other books, and at least one appropriate religious painting; Thanksgiving or other holiday guests from some other nationality, race, or cultural group.

— Arrange youth-parents meetings—a youth-parents panel, role-playing with young people playing the part of parents, and parents playing the part of youth. Discuss use of auto, allowance, clothes, dates, hours, TV, studying, school and church functions, the family council.

— Make special use of Christian Education Week, Youth Week, and Christian Family Week to strengthen home ties. Emphasize family-stay-at-home nights.

— Conduct family nights at church with special programs and family fun together.

Fellowship in recreation

— Arrange a recreation workshop, or coaching clinic; or send representatives to an area conference or recreation laboratory.

— Discuss Christian ideals for recreation, and develop a "Christian Code for Recreation" or "Ten Commandments for Sportsmanship."

— Create an "Idea Book for Recreation," or a file of games, party and banquet suggestions, etc. Establish a recreation bookshelf.

— Make up a "Recreation Calendar for the Year," with appropriate parties, banquets, outings, and other recreation events. Plan one event for each month, or as may be required—for example, Fall Kickoff Banquet, Halloween, Hobby Night, Christmas Festival, New Year's Eve Party, Valentine Party, etc.

— Emphasize outdoor recreation throughout the year, and provide for various types of sport, some of them suitable for mixed groups—roller skating, ice skating, bowling, volley ball, ping-pong, croquet, tennis, swimming, softball, deck tennis, darts, shuffleboard, miniature golf, etc.

— Develop leisure activities. Start hobbies (such as stamps, records, shells, minerals, flowers, leaves, fossils, pictures, coins, buttons, books, autographs, china, butterflies). Establish hobby clubs and hobby fairs. Use hobby collections for worship centers (shells, stones, books, crosses, leaves, flowers, pictures) and for discussion meetings.

— Establish a book club (poetry, novels, plays, biography, travel, etc.) or a music appreciation club (recordings of symphonies, musicals, operas, ballads, folk music, etc.).

— Develop a game room, or youth center, and equip it with table games and other facilities for recreation.

— Start a "make-it-yourself" group, with adult assistance, creating useful articles for home and church use (bookshelves, picture frames, curtains, drapes, cabinets, toys and equipment for children, etc.).

— Develop creative activity interest groups—poster making, mimeographing (including art work and lettering), ceramics, copper work, plastics, woodwork and carpentry, leatherwork, bookbinding, puppets, textile painting, spatter painting, clay modeling, murals, electrical and mechanical work.

— Provide opportunities for appreciation of drama—role-playing, play reading, walk-on rehearsals, stunts and skits, wire or tape recordings, charades, choral reading (for fun as well as for worship), patomimes, tableaux.

— Use folk games, and other singing games.

— Have talent nights for readings, dramatic acts, musical performances, etc.

THE PROGRAM OF RECREATION

Like other elements in the educational program, the recreational activity, to hold interest and to accomplish the best results, must be graded. Fortunately, many types of recreation have general appeal to all ages of youth, though certain types may have decreasing or increasing appeal as young people mature. As mental growth takes place and physical skill expands, social interest likewise broadens; especially i there marked increase in interest in those of the opposite sex Accordingly, the distinctive aims vary with the different age groups under consideration, even though they are applied to similar activities.

Junior high

For example, junior highs, who are undergoing extensive and disturbing physical changes, need many opportunities for active recreation to release energy, to develop their muscles, and to acquire fundamental skills in different kinds of sports in which they will become more proficient later. They need to try many different active games and athletic contests so as to improve many different muscles. They need to know the exhilaration, excitement, and challenge of abundant physical life. But they also have other needs, which cannot safely be neglected. Their physical awkwardness, resulting from rapid and sometimes uneven physical development, is paralleled, for many, by their social awkwardness. The awakening of interest in the opposite sex, accompanied by dawning self-consciousness, and often by great emotional instability and an inner sense of insecurity, may express itself in a variety of ways – aggressive behavior, loud talking, teasing, giggling, play-acting, and "limelight seeking," or even by withdrawal behavior (because of fear or insecurity).

Among the aims of recreation with junior highs should be these — to provide constructive outlets for self-expression; to offer substitutes for unacceptable ways of seeking recognition; to assist in creating confidence, restraint, and control. Play is a great equalizer. It offers an immediate channel for merging self with the group. Self-control, co-operation, courtesy, tolerance, forbearance, comradeship, fair play — these are but a few of the expansive social qualities which play can help to foster.

In planning a balanced and effective recreation program for the two or three junior high years, the church leaders should show the same educational insight — attention to meaningful detail and to specific character objectives for each event

— as for planning worship or study. Outdoor life, nature craft, hobbies, athletic skills, and active games should predominate. Formal parties based upon adult patterns, requiring adult dress and late hours, should be minimized. Yet, there should be adequate opportunity for socializing, and for initial experiences in learning how to eat in public; to play parlor games, now and then with partners; to date for parties; and to discover special cultural interests in music, literature, drama, and creative art. Thus recreation may help junior highs to live more abundant lives, and may contribute to growth in Christian character.

Senior high .

With senior highs the needs for physical, mental, and social development through recreation are similar to those of junior highs, but at a more advanced level. In athletics and active games, there is more refinement of skill, more muscle tone and strength, better co-ordination and timing. For the church's athletic program, there is opportunity to encourage wholesome boy-girl relationship through such activities as swimming, volley ball, softball, tennis, ping-pong, shuffle board, skating, hikes, horseback riding, bicycling. In social events there is opportunity to assist in developing the social graces — poise; courtesy; consideration of others; ease in conversation; personal charm and wit; skill in parlor games; self-expression through music, charades, stunts, and other forms of entertainment. The Christian basis for politeness, friendliness, and considerate social behavior needs to be understood. Help is needed on such problems as "How to become datable," "What to do on a date," "Christian standards for recreation." Opportunities may be provided for the development of special skills in art and poster-making, lettering, creative crafts, writing, drama, etc.

It is not necessary for the church to duplicate or imitate all that is being done elsewhere, but rather to set its own standards and build its own plans, to minister to unmet needs, to guide youth in making choices of recreation and leisure activity, to enrich personal lives at the point of need, and to provide a balanced, church-centered program.

Business young people and students

For older youth the recreation program should be diversified and challenging, well planned and appealing. By this time most young people have many interests and opportunities. The church should stand for a quality of fellowship which is distinctive. Recreation should be consistent with Christian ideals. Concern should be felt for each member of the group, for his or her adjustment to others, and for a maximum development of personality. Few churches can compete successfully with commercialized amusements operated on their own professional basis. It is not smart to try. But many churches have demonstrated that it is possible to put such a friendly, personalized spirit into their recreation program as to lead employed young people and students to choose the church as a center for their social life, and to realize the church's place in balanced living.

Students vary much as to the demands made upon their time. Most campus-related Student Fellowships find that there is a real need for fellowship among Christian youth, yet difficulty in finding time for it. Students who are daily or weekend commuters may be able to maintain close association with the local church by sharing in some of its social events, as well as in some on the campus. Rural youth, with long hours of work, may take advantage of seasonal opportunities when work is lighter. Employed youth, likewise busy, are also in need of church-centered recreation.

CHAPTER X

LEADERSHIP

"Follow me and I will make you become . . ." [1]

QUALIFICATIONS FOR CHRISTIAN LEADERSHIP

A genuine interest in persons

Christian leadership differs from other leadership chiefly in that it is person-centered. Its aim is not to dominate or use persons but to help them find the abundant life. The first qualification of a Christian leader is a genuine and abiding interest in individual persons. He must show young people that he really believes in them, has faith in their potentialities, likes to be with them and is willing to expend himself if necessary in order that true Christian personality may be developed in them.

A radiant and contagious personal religious experience

The starting point with others is a genuine Christian experience in oneself. There must be spiritual rootage in God and visible evidence of continuing growth in the Christian life, if others are to be helped in finding a life of faith. It is of the utmost importance for young people that their leaders reveal in their faces, their voices, and their actions a quality of Christian life which is radiant and contagious. This does not mean superficial exuberance and casual optimism, indifference to the grim realities of contemporary life. On the contrary, it is those persons who have lived most, suffered and felt the most, and who still reveal a joyous faith, who most deeply influence young people.

[1] Mark 1:17.

A clear sense of purpose—ability to define goals and measure progress

An adult or a young person can feel the lift which comes from a sense of divine mission. This may come first from discovering a need to be filled in working with youth in the church; next, from feeling that with God's help we can fill that need; and finally, from giving ourselves heartily to the task in a true spirit of dedication. Of all the satisfactions of life, there are none greater than those which come when one responds to the will of God and achieves a measure of success in the spiritual guidance of youth.

The devoted leader of youth will be constantly seeking not only for a clear purpose for his own life but also for sharply defined goals for his youth group. The ability to define goals for oneself in working with youth from month to month and year to year, and the ability to help young people in defining tangible and achievable goals for themselves individually and as a group — these are among the qualifications important to success. The tests of progress are sometimes specific — enrollment and attendance, units of study completed, projects undertaken. Often they deal with the intangibles — a change in spirit, a new sense of commitment, an appreciation of others, a deeper understanding of the Christian faith and its application to life today.

A working knowledge of the Christian faith—"know-how" in youth work

There are a number of things which the youth leader must seek to learn. He needs a fund of usable knowledge about the Bible, Christian history and doctrine, Christian literature, the missionary enterprise, the application of the Christian gospel to personal and social problems of today, the sources for help. He also needs "know-how" in church work with youth. This means that he should make good use of manuals on organization and method, curricular and program materials, audio-visuals and other aids. It means, likewise, that eventually he should be well-versed in business and planning procedures, in adolescent psychology, in tested methods of teaching, in the newer developments in group dynamics as applied to youth meetings and planning sessions. Those who work with junior highs will find knowledge of creative crafts and hobbies and of weekday club organizations and activities (the Scouts, Camp Fire Girls, 4-H, the Y programs, etc.) of value, especially if these are seen in the perspective of the current move toward a unified, church-centered program. Knowledge and skill in recreation leadership will prove valuable, especially with senior and junior highs. A familiarity with sacred music and great Christian hymns, with religious art and poetry, with biography and literature, with the resources for worship, is highly desirable. Leaders of employed older youth and students need, ideally, to get acquainted with many fields of thought — science, philosophy, history, psychology, literature, sociology, for example — which influence the thought and life of those with whom they work, and to be able to assist in the selection of topics, study units, and resource materials.

No leader can expect to start with full knowledge in all these fields, or ever to become fully versed in every realm which has value to his task. There is great satisfaction in the awareness that real progress can be made in a reasonable period of time by anyone who starts with a good foundation of basic knowledge and makes use of the many opportunities furnished by libraries, schools, broadcasting stations, and conferences with other leaders. The leadership education curricula of your denomination and the National Council of Churches provide excellent courses and texts in a wide variety of fields which should be made available to workers in every church and community through training classes, institutes, workshops, and coaching sessions.

The ability to inspire

No worker with young people has reached the highest level of leadership unless he has developed the ability to inspire youth. This is a particularly vital qualification for one who deals with a religion of such vast potentialities as Christianity. Routine activity and smoothly functioning programs are not enough. The Christian gospel is a life-transforming force which needs to be set at work in the lives of young people to help them to become the best of which they are capable, with Christ's help. The Christian leader of youth should seek to learn when to give a word of encouragement, when to get excited, when to praise, when to prod a young person into greater accomplishment. He should be able to help young people to dream dreams and to make those dreams come true.

CHARACTERISTICS OF SUCCESSFUL LEADERSHIP OF YOUTH

Spiritual depth

No clever bag of tricks or dependence upon persuasive personality traits and techniques of group leadership can be a substitute for spiritual depth in church work with youth. The Christian leader of youth must himself have lived and felt deeply. He should have thought his way through many disturbing questions such as those which plague youth. He needs the ability to look deeply into the inner life and motivation of those with whom he works and to make correct diagnoses of spiritual needs. Even more, he must be able to assist youth in applying to their problems answers which really make a difference.

Emotional maturity

In the typical youth group — particularly junior or senior highs — emotional problems are likely to emerge from time to time — love affairs, crushes, jealousies, tensions, sensitiveness. Junior highs may be quite moody; one moment elated and happy, the next depressed. Among seniors some may feel neglected, discriminated against. And older youth are by no means exempt from sudden emotional impulses and immaturities. Most good adult leaders have experienced enough of life to be understanding about emotional problems and excesses. On the one hand, they can respond emotionally, with tenderness and warmth, to the finest conduct; on the other hand, with restrained indignation, to wrongdoing. They can assist young people to outgrow infantilisms. They can help in recognizing and rejecting moods of pessimism, selfishness and pettiness; in restraining undue emotional expression in boy-girl relationships; in responding to high moments of spiritual exaltation; and in keeping a wholesome balance between intellect and feeling. Such opportunities are always challenging.

A sense of humor

This quality, so essential for success with youth, is useful in relieving tension, in restoring balance, in promoting good rapport, in building group spirit. A skillful leader — by a well-chosen story or a clever remark — can enliven discussion, create a feeling of good fellowship, speed up the pace of group planning, and increase interest. Though humor may be a gift with some, it is quite possible for a leader with limited natural talent for humor to cultivate this ability, thus improving himself at this point.

Of the many types of humor, often the most effective is slow, dry wit. A shy, halting manner disarms any feeling of resentment, or envy of polish and brilliance. A good-humored, friendly person, wanting others to feel at ease and to enjoy themselves, may find laughter and good feeling in very ordinary situations and in the remarks of others. Abusing humor — stimulating too much levity and horseplay — is dangerous. There is risk in humor when it becomes an end in itself; in heavy-handed humor that misses the point, or is poorly timed; in humor that is really sarcasm, and carries a sting.

To say that every adult counselor should have a sense of humor does not mean that he must be the life of the party. The wise leader will study himself and his group, and learn how to use humor as an effective tool.

Imagineering

"Imagineering" is "the art of thinking about the future while your hands are busy with the present, the ability to let your imagination soar and then to engineer it down to earth, the stuff out of which the future for which we are working will ultimately be made." It is a particularly appropriate and vital trait for the leader of Christian youth to possess, since Christianity is a combination of the ideal and the real, the visionary and the practical. An effective leader of church work with youth should be capable of insight and imagination. "Where there is no vision, the people perish . . ." (Prov. 29:18 KJV). Likewise, the leader should have a talent for accomplishment, an awareness of the importance of detailed planning of programs and projects, and an ability to follow through. He should seek to be a social engineer, building personal lives and group spirit upon the foundation of Jesus Christ. This foundation must ever be kept in mind: "For no other foundation can anyone lay than that which is laid, which is Jesus Christ" (1 Cor. 3:11).

FUNCTIONS OF THE LEADER

The role of the adult leader of youth

The leader as counselor and friend. The first need of most young people is for a sympathetic, understanding friend. An adult who can be a good listener, a helpful adviser, a skillful counselor, will have a real place in the affection and respect of young people. There are various levels, as well as various techniques, of counseling. The professionally qualified counselor is one who has had thorough training, usually a graduate degree for specialized training in this field, and is equipped to deal with deep psychological disturbances. Only those who are professionally qualified should seek to counsel on this level. At the other extreme is the elementary level of counseling which involves referral to a source of help. The referral may be to a school counselor, a vocational guidance expert, a physician, a marriage counselor, a psychiatrist, or a minister, depending upon what the need is. Some real knowledge and insight are required even at the most elementary level, if the right suggestions are to be offered.

Through reading, study courses, and experience, many lay adult leaders of youth may equip themselves for a secondary level of counseling. This is the level of assistance with the common problems faced by typical, normal young people. The great majority of young people — if they are to find help at all upon the many questions which disturb them as they move from childhood through early, middle, and later adolescence to adulthood — must gain this help from parents, teachers, and other lay counselors. It is important that the adult leader become equipped to offer help of a sound, constructive nature in such fields as personal commitment to Christ, church membership, prayer, understanding of the Bible and the Christian faith, sex, boy-girl relationships,

Christian ideals of love and marriage, personality adjustments, spiritual growth, emotional maturity, vocational motivation and opportunities, personal standards and ideals.

The need in counseling is for more than knowledge and advice; it is for skill in helping young people to help themselves. Most professional counselors emphasize the "non-directive" or "non-aggressive" attitude.

The leader as teacher and guide. Teaching is most certainly one form of leadership. The guidance of the thinking of young people in formal class sessions calls for a high degree of skill. It should result in increased knowledge and changed attitudes; also, in Christian conduct and a new way of life. It should likewise influence group planning of meetings and action projects, as we have seen in Chapter IV on "The Planning Process." In all these varied ways, the teacher is a leader.

The leader as administrator — organizer and planner. The Youth Fellowship advisers and other leaders who have executive responsibilities must study their task and its relationship to the Youth Fellowship officers, who also have executive responsibility. First, it is desirable to survey the responsibilities and functions which relate to the effective administration of youth work in the Christian church; then, to determine how these are best shared or divided among the adult leaders and the youth officers. The responsibilities include: (1) presiding over planning sessions and committee meetings; (2) conducting business meetings; (3) preparing agenda for such meetings; (4) appointing special committees; (5) following through on plans; (6) checking up on officers and committees; (7) reporting on progress; (8) leadership of classes; (9) leadership of discussion meetings and worship sessions; (10) leadership of parties and action projects; (11) promotion of fellowship events; (12) relationships to parents; (13) relationships to church school leaders, to church boards, and to workers with other age groups.

The degree of adult responsibility and initiative which is desirable will vary widely with the different age groups. With older youth the adviser is primarily an experienced person who sits in on the planning, and is available to offer suggestions, to raise questions, to assure continuity in planning, and to explore resources. With senior highs the adviser should be in close touch with all that is happening without dominating it, should be free to add his suggestions, and now and then to make recommendations (if not too often), and should be so much an accepted part of the group that his advice is sought after when needed, and respected when offered. With junior highs there is need for more guidance, but without its being too conspicuous or comprehensive. The adult adviser must develop skill in helping junior highs to do their own organizing and planning, to analyze and appraise as they discuss, and to seek the mature judgment of their leader only when it is needed.

The role of the young person who is a leader

Building spirit — enlisting interest and action. In enlisting the interest and building the spirit of a youth group, no adult can equal the effectiveness of a young person who is their own age. Some young people have a natural flare for doing just these things; some may have to be taught how to develop and use leadership traits. The fact that young people have been elected or appointed by the will of the group to lead should usually carry with it a sense of confidence and reasonable assurance of support. An obligation is laid upon the leader to enlist help through what Trecker calls "responsible participation." "Responsible participation is characterized by the willing contribution of one's ideas, experiences, opinions, and beliefs. . . . [It] means an acceptance and follow-through on interim assignments." [2]

The young person who is an officer or leader should not abuse his position by misusing his leadership for selfish purposes, or by defaulting on his responsibilities. He should regard his tasks as a leader in church work with youth as second to none in importance, and should use all his powers of personality to inspire co-operation, to enlist full participation, and to create a strong sense of teamwork and dedication to the task. One advantage in passing the jobs around, especially in the younger groups, is the training in leadership supplied for many, and the feeling that all may have a responsible part.

Leading business sessions. Young people who put their minds to it may quickly learn how to conduct business sessions in an orderly way. The first necessity is an order of business; then, an adherence to good parliamentary procedure. Some young people have taken real satisfaction in drilling one another in Robert's *Rules of Order:* how to present a motion . . . how to conduct votes . . . which motions are in order, and which have priority. It is good discipline and training for junior highs to learn how to maintain order; address the chair; state motions clearly; respect minority rights; and decide issues by majority votes. Older youth who learn democratic parliamentary procedures in Youth Fellowship business meetings will find these helpful as they assume adult responsibilities. However, it should be realized that Robert's *Rules of Order* are simply a means to attain orderliness and insure fair play. A Christian group is bound by a higher rule, the law of love (as expressed, for example, in the Golden Rule) found in the New Testament and in the spirit

[2] From *Group Process in Administration,* by Harleigh B. Trecker. Copyright, 1946, 1950, by Whiteside, Inc. Used by permission.

of Jesus; hence, it should show courtesy and consideration in an attempt to find the will of God, and should not become too legalistic in spirit.

Conducting committee meetings. Since so many of us spend so much of our life in committee meetings, it is important for us to learn while we are young how to conduct such meetings successfully. The leadership of the youth chairman is important, and each member of the committee must assume his share of responsibility. The chairman has a number of responsibilities: (1) setting clear goals for the meetings (usually with the help of a docket or agenda); (2) keeping discussion on the topic; (3) making sure everyone keeps alert, and contributes his best ideas; (4) helping to clear up differences (not by riding roughshod over anyone, but by full discussion until there is a meeting of minds; or, if necessary, a vote); (5) assisting in bringing discussion speedily to decision (so as to accomplish as much as possible in a minimum of time); (6) seeing that accurate records are kept; (7) fixing responsibility for action, in harmony with decisions reached; (8) checking up on accomplishment. It is often possible in committee meetings to speed up action through elimination of a formal vote by announcing, "If there is no objection we will consider it settled that . . ." or "If we are all agreed . . . we will move on to the next problem." If formal voting seems advisable, the chairman's leadership can often be of help through the use of three questions: 1. Before there is a motion . . . "Is someone ready to make a motion?" 2. After a motion is presented . . . "Is the motion clear?" 3. After discussion . . . "Are we ready to vote on the motion?"

Handling planning — making plans and people work. Much more is involved for the leader than the committee meetings themselves. He must have a clear idea of what his own job is, and of the purpose of the committee which he leads. He must be on the lookout for ideas and possible plans, think his way through the various possibilities, and encourage his committee members to do likewise. All this comes before the meeting, and as background for building his agenda. After the meeting, comes the work of seeing the decisions through to successful action. Here, leadership may be required in enlisting help, in promoting co-operation and dependability, in seeing that the job is done well. Sometimes the leader may have to do more than his share of the work; plans may have to be modified, if they are to work; people may have to be prodded and pushed and coaxed to get them started, and then checked up on repeatedly.

TECHNIQUES OF EFFECTIVE LEADERSHIP

Working behind the scenes

In church work with youth, indirect leadership is more successful in the long run than direct. "Leadership from the rear" characterizes the adviser, whose aim is to develop leadership traits among those he serves. A review of the functions of leaders mentioned previously in the section on "The leader as administrator" will confirm the observation that most of those mentioned are primarily responsibilities of the youth officer rather than the adult adviser — for example, presiding over meetings, preparing agenda, leadership of worship, parties, projects, etc. This applies in considerable measure to junior highs, and certainly to seniors and older youth. Yet, there is a responsibility of the adult adviser to exert leadership of a skillful nature with respect to each of these functions. Though he does not preside, he does teach young people how to do so well. He may review issues and problems in advance, and raise questions or offer pointers concerning ways of handling them. He may hold an informal "postmortem," now and then, to discuss "how it might be done even better next time." He may help plan the agenda in advance, with the president or chairman, and make comments ahead of time so as to reduce the necessity of his participating too frequently in the meetings. He may have many helpful conferences with those who are to lead discussion meetings, worship services, fellowship events, or projects; and may provide helpful books, magazines, and other resources, as well as personal advice and tips.

Delegating responsibility—developing leaders

Both for adult leaders of youth and for youth leaders of youth, a prime consideration is that responsibility be delegated, that jobs be passed around, that many have a chance to try their hand at various tasks. This is not only to maintain interest; it is also to discover and develop leadership potentialities in as many of the young people as possible. One reason why it is desirable to change officers frequently with junior highs, and to have no standing committees, is that they are still at the stage of finding themselves and discovering their abilities. Some may be too eager to try, and may not prove dependable; others may be reluctant, and have to be pressed. It is essential that all the tasks, great and small, be treated with respect. They are part of the work of Christ; hence, sacred missions. Much patient consideration may need to be given to emphasize this fact. The quality of dependability, so essential in all leadership, needs to be strengthened among the young people of the group.

Encouraging the good

There is merit with young people, as with adults, in "accentuating the positive." Although correction of the bad is often necessary, and sin, wrongdoing, and error must be faced in every life, the basic state of the Christian life is one in which the door is always wide open to the good. This applies not only to purity of thought and to moral behavior but also to quality of achievement. The effective leader knows the value of encouragement in promoting confidence. He finds a little talent which he may commend, and through encouragement helps it to grow.

LEARNING THE ART OF LEADERSHIP FROM JESUS

Seeing persons through the eyes of Jesus

Those early disciples were much like young people today — impulsive, unreliable Peter; skeptical Nathanael; doubting Thomas; ambitious James and John; preoccupied Martha; impractical Mary. In each of these, Jesus saw a person with spiritual needs and potentialities; for each he made himself available; to each he supplied help as he said, "I came that they may have life, and have it abundantly" (John 10:10). Such a leader as Jesus has never been known. He set the example by his words of encouragement and faith, by the way in which he transformed humble fishermen into disciples, themselves world transformers.

How Jesus developed leadership

Jesus spent time with his disciples, individually and as a group. He sought them out and encouraged them to commit their lives, without reservation, to him. He discovered and developed traits in them which they did not know they possessed. He set up a school of leadership, gave them definite assignments of work to do to test their skill, and then arranged coaching sessions for appraisal and further instructions. From this process came a close-knit fellowship which transformed a small company of ordinary men into a force which has changed the course of history. The youth adviser today should study the ways in which Jesus developed leadership, and seek to apply them reverently but courageously to his own group. What happened then can happen again — with His help — in the lives of modern youth.

FINDING AND DEVELOPING LEADERSHIP

When Margaret Slattery said, "It may be true that teachers are born; but they are not born made," [3] she spoke truth which applies to all leaders. Many have potentialities for lay leadership of youth who are unaware of it, or who are letting assignments of lesser importance clutter up their lives. The first task is to find these leaders. There are such in almost every congregation — understanding parents, reliable persons engaged in business, professional men and women, teachers, recent college graduates with courses in psychology and other fields, skilled craftsmen with alert minds and dependable traits. In co-operation with the church board of Christian education, such persons must be found, their qualifications reviewed, and steps taken to enlist their help. Fortunately, there are many ways to assist them in developing knowledge and skill. Coaching procedures should include the reading of at least one good book or manual in each of the major fields, such as teaching methods, the church and its functioning, Youth Fellowship organization and program, the Old Testament, the New Testament, the life and teachings of Jesus. Observation of other churches, and conferences with other leaders, are of great value; also, participation in standard leadership education classes in the local church or in interchurch schools.

[3] From *You Can Learn to Teach,* by Margaret Slattery. Copyright, 1925. The Pilgrim Press. Used by permission.

RESOURCES FOR GROWTH IN LEADERSHIP

It is apparent that the effective leader of youth must be a resourceful person, and that there is constant room for growth in this challenging task. Hence, the need for resources. Ideally, the church should provide many of these for the youth department bookcase, the church library, or for use in the home of the leader. For suggestions, see the bibliography in this book. A careful selection on a "book-of-the-month" basis should in due time bring the average reader up to date in many of the fields represented in youth leadership. Young people, themselves, should be encouraged to read many of these books, and to hold briefing and coaching sessions dealing with various books and manuals.

Other resources for growth in leadership are also available. These include the annual retreat, the monthly workers' conference or workshop, the area conferences and coaching sessions, the spiritual disciplines of daily prayer and Bible study, regular worship and service, association with stimulating personalities through personal conversation, or through their writings and their biographies. The broader the knowledge and appreciation, and the deeper the experience and understanding, the greater will be the influence of the Christian leader upon those whose lives may, in turn, influence many others.

This book is written in the great hope that thus, through youth, the Christian fellowship itself may find new life, and may take a new place of vigorous leadership, in the thoughts and relationship of persons the world over.

SELECTED BIBLIOGRAPHY

HELPS IN PLANNING AND ADMINISTRATION

Baptist Youth Fellowship. *Baptist Youth Fellowship Handbook.* B.Y.F. Philadelphia.

Barbar, Estelle. *Guiding Intermediates in Worship.* Abingdon-Cokesbury Press. New York. 1946.

Bays, Alice A. *Worship Programs and Stories for Young People.* Abingdon-Cokesbury Press. New York. 1948.

————. *Worship Services for Life Planning.* Abingdon-Cokesbury Press. New York. 1953.

————. *Services for Teen-agers.* Abingdon-Cokesbury Press. New York. 1954.

Beckes, Isaac. *Young Leaders in Action.* Abingdon-Cokesbury Press. New York. 1941.

Bowman, Clarice M. *Guiding Intermediates.* Abingdon-Cokesbury Press. New York. 1943.

————. *Restoring Worship.* Abingdon-Cokesbury Press. New York. 1951.

Brown, Thelma. *Treasury of Religious Plays.* Association Press. New York. 1947.

Coyle, G. L. *Group Work with American Youth.* Harper & Brothers. New York. 1948.

Currie, Bettie (ed.). *Handbook: Senior High Fellowship.* John Knox Press. Richmond. 1952.

Cummings, Oliver deWolf. *Christian Education in the Local Church.* The Judson Press. Philadelphia. 1942.

Emurian, Ernest K. *More Dramatized Stories of Hymns and Hymn Writers.* W. A. Wilde Company. Boston. 1943.

Fordham, Forrest B. *Our Church Plans for Youth.* The Judson Press. Philadelphia. 1953.

Griffiths, Louise B. *Missionary Education for the Junior High School Age.* Friendship Press. New York. 1948.

Harbin, E. O. *The Recreation Leader.* Abingdon-Cokesbury Press. New York. 1952.

Harrison, Russell F. *This is CYF.* Christian Board of Publication. St. Louis. 1954. New York. 1939.

Harner, N. C. *Missionary Education in Your Church*. Friendship Press. New York. 1942.

——. *Youth Work in the Church*. Abingdon-Cokesbury Press. New York. 1942.

Hoiland, Richard. *The Young People's Meeting*. The Judson Press. Philadelphia. 1943.

Lotz, P. H. (ed.) *Orientation in Religious Education*. Abingdon-Cokesbury Press. New York. 1950.

Maus, Cynthia P. *Christ and the Fine Arts*. Harper & Brothers. New York. 1938.

——. *The World's Great Madonnas*. Harper & Brothers. New York. 1947.

Mayer, Herbert C. *Young People in Your Church*. Fleming H. Revell Co. Westwood, N. J. 1953.

Moon, Alleen. *The Christian Education of Older Youth*. Abingdon-Cokesbury Press. New York. 1943.

Rich, Mark, et al. *Youth Work in the Rural Church*. Christian Board of Publication. St. Louis. 1940.

Roberts, Dorothy M. *Leadership of Teen-Age Groups*. Association Press. New York. 1950.

Schroeder, Ruth. *Youth Programs for Special Occasions*. Abingdon-Cokesbury Press. New York. 1950.

Strauss, Bert and Frances. *New Ways to Better Meetings*. The Viking Press. New York. 1951.

Tower, H. E. *Church Use of Audio-Visuals*. Abingdon-Cokesbury Press. New York. 1951.

Vieth, Paul (ed.). *The Church and Christian Education*. The Bethany Press. St. Louis. 1947.

Wilcox, Jackson. *Junior High Advisers' Handbook*. Baptist Youth Fellowship. Philadelphia. 1952.

Youth Department. *Handbook of the Methodist Youth Fellowship*. The Methodist Publishing House. Nashville. 1953.

Youth Department. *Guild Guide* (Handbook on the Fellowship Guild of the B.Y.F.). Baptist Youth Fellowship. Philadelphia.

UNDERSTANDING YOUTH AND THEIR NEEDS

Adams, Clifford R. *Looking Ahead to Marriage*. Science Research Associates. Chicago. 1949.

Brown, Alberta. *The 7 Teen Years*. The Bethany Press. St. Louis. 1954.

Burkhart, Roy. *Understanding Youth*. Abingdon-Cokesbury Press. New York. 1938.

Burkhart, Roy, and Jean Hamm. *Making Our Friendships Christian*. The Judson Press. Philadelphia. 1952.

Crawford, J. E., and L. E. Woodward. *Better Ways of Growing Up*. Muhlenberg Press. Philadelphia. 1948.

Dahlberg, E. T. *Youth and the Homes of Tomorrow*. The Judson Press. Philadelphia. 1934.

Dickerson, Roy. *Understanding Myself*. Association Press. New York. 1940.

Duvall, E. R. M. *Facts of Life and Love*. Association Press. New York. 1940.

————. *Keeping Up With the Teen-Agers*. Public Affairs Pamphlets No. 127. Washington. 1947.

Duvall, E. R. M., and R. L. Hill. *When You Marry*. Association Press. New York. 1945.

Ferguson, Rowena. *Teen-Agers—Their Days and Ways*. National Council of the Churches of Christ in the U.S.A. Chicago. 1952.

Gregor, Arthur S. *Time Out for Youth*. The Macmillan Company. New York. 1951.

Harner, N. C. *About Myself*. Christian Education Press. Philadelphia. 1950.

Harris, Erdman. *Introduction to Youth*. The Macmillan Company. New York. 1940.

Humphreys, J. Anthony. *Choosing Your Career*. Science Research Associates. Chicago. 1949.

Jenkins, Gladys Gardner, and Joy Newman. *How to Live With Parents*. Science Research Association. 1950.

Kirkendall, Lester A., and Ruth Farnum Osborne. *Dating Days*. Science Research Associates. Chicago. 1948.

Kuder, G. Frederick, and Blanche B. Paulson. *Discovering Your Real Interests*. Science Research Associates. Chicago. 1948.

Sweeney, Esther Emerson. *Dates and Dating*. Woman's Press. New York. 1948.

Weitzman, Ellis. *Growing Up Socially*. Science Research Associates. Chicago. 1948.

Wuttenberg, Rudolph. *On Call for Youth*. Association Press. New York. 1955.

HELPING YOUTH TO UNDERSTAND THE BIBLE AND THE CHRISTIAN FAITH

Anderson, B. W. *Rediscovering the Bible.* Association Press. New York. 1951.

Bailey, Albert E. *Daily Life in Bible Times.* Charles Scribner's Sons. New York. 1943.

Bro, Margueritte Harmon. *Every Day a Prayer.* Harper & Brothers. New York. 1943.

————. *More Than We Are.* Harper & Brothers. New York. 1948.

Buttrick, George. *Prayer.* Abingdon-Cokesbury Press. New York. 1942.

Calhoun, Robert Lowry. *God and the Day's Work.* Association Press. New York. 1943.

Casteel, John L. *Rediscovering Prayer.* Association Press. New York. 1955.

Ferrari, Erma Paul. *God in My Vocation.* The Judson Press. Philadelphia. 1949.

Finegan, Jack. *Light from the Ancient Past.* Princeton University Press. Princeton. 1946.

Goodspeed, Edgar J. *How to Read the Bible.* John C. Winston Company. Philadelphia. 1946.

Harner, N. C. *I Believe.* Christian Education Press. Philadelphia. 1950.

Hayward, Percy. *Young People's Prayers.* Association Press. New York. 1945.

Hordern, William. *A Layman's Guide to Protestant Theology.* The Macmillan Company. New York. 1955.

Jones, E. Stanley. *Mastery—The Art of Mastering Life.* Abingdon-Cokesbury Press. New York. 1955.

Jordan, Clarence. *Sermon on the Mount.* The Judson Press. Philadelphia. 1955.

Mathews, Basil. *Forward Through the Ages.* Friendship Press. New York. 1951.

Nelson, John Oliver, (ed.) *The Student Prayerbook.* Association Press. New York. 1953.

Nelson, J. Robert. *The Christian Student and the Church.* Association Press. New York. 1952.

————. *The Christian Student and the World Struggle.* Association Press. New York. 1952.

Nichols, James Hastings. *Primer for Protestants.* Association Press. New York. 1947.

Niles, Daniel. *Reading the Bible Today*. Association Press. New York
1955.

Ross, Murray. *The Religious Beliefs of Youth*. Association Press. New
York. 1950.

Seifert, Harvey. *Fellowships of Concern*. Abingdon-Cokesbury Press. New
York. 1949.

Trueblood, Elton. *Alternative to Futility*. Harper & Brothers. New York
1948.

————. *The Common Ventures of Life*. Harper & Brothers. New
York. 1949.

————. *Your Other Vocation*. Harper & Brothers. New York. 1953.

Wickenden, Arthur. *Youth Looks at Religion*. Harper & Brothers. New
York. 1948.

AIDS IN TEACHING AND COUNSELING YOUTH

Bailey, Albert E. *Jesus and His Teachings; the Approach Through Art*
Christian Education Press. Philadelphia. 1942.

————. *Christ and His Gospel in Recent Art*. Charles Scribner's Sons
New York. 1948.

Berkeley, James P. *You Can Teach*. The Judson Press. Philadelphia
1941.

Bowman, Clarice M. *Ways Youth Learn*. Harper & Brothers. New York
1952.

Cober, K. L., and E. Stricker. *Teaching Seniors*. The Judson Press. Phila
delphia. 1940.

Cummings, Oliver deWolf. *Guiding Youth in Christian Growth*. The
Judson Press. Philadelphia. 1954.

Cutton, G. L. *Teaching Young People*. The Judson Press. Philadelphia
1941.

Desjardins, Lucile. *Teaching Intermediates*. The Judson Press. Phila
delphia. 1940.

Eakin, Mildred and Frank. *The Church School Teacher's Job*. The
Macmillan Company. 1949.

Haiman, Franklyn S. *Group Leadership and Democratic Action*. Hough
ton Mifflin Company. Boston. 1951.

May, Rollo. *The Art of Counseling*. Abingdon-Cokesbury Press. New
York. 1939.

Miller, R. C. *The Clue to Christian Education*. Charles Scribner's Sons
New York. 1950.

2 $\frac{50}{91}$